The Siege of Ladysmith

Gerald Sharp

MACDONALD AND JANE'S · LONDON

Copyright © 1976 Gerald Sharp
First published in 1976 by
Macdonald and Jane's Publishers Limited
Paulton House
8 Shepherdess Walk
London N1 7LW

Printed and bound in Great Britain by
REDWOOD BURN LIMITED
Trowbridge & Esher

ISBN 0 356 08346 2

CONTENTS

CHAPTER ONE
The Background: Why War Came

THE outbreak of war between Britain and the Boer Republics in 1899 was the consequence of fundamental differences in the way of life and outlook of the two peoples. To Britain the Cape of Good Hope was primarily a staging-post on the route to India. The Boers had no such Imperial preoccupations. They wanted to be left alone and resented their dependence on Britain and Portugal for access to the sea. Britain and the Boers also had different policies towards the African tribes.

In 1877 Britain annexed the Transvaal, at that time an impoverished and backward state. Three years later the Transvaalers revolted. The result was the First Boer War, which ended in February, 1881 with the defeat of the British at Majuba Hill in Northern Natal. Britain subsequently granted independence to the Transvaal while claiming to exercise 'suzerainty' over the Republic, which the latter disputed.

In 1886 extensive gold deposits were discovered in the Transvaal and made the Republic's fortune overnight. Uitlanders, as the Boers called foreigners, came in their thousands to work the goldfields and eventually outnumbered the Transvaal burghers. Like the Boers they had to pay taxes, but were excluded from any share in the government of the country; as most of the Uitlanders were British, their complaints further poisoned relationships between Britain and the Transvaal.

A crisis arose at the end of 1895 when Dr Jameson attempted a raid on Johannesburg in support of the Uitlanders' grievances. The raid was a fiasco, and a serious embarrass-

1

ment to the British Government which disowned Jameson before knowing whether it had succeeded. To the Boers, the raid was proof of Britain's hostile intentions; they were already buying arms in Europe, and these purchases were stepped up.

In May 1899 a conference on the status of the Uitlanders in the Transvaal was held at Bloemfontein, capital of the Orange Free State, attended by President Kruger of the Transvaal and the British High Commissioner at the Cape, Sir Alfred Milner. It ended in deadlock, for the attitudes of the Uitlanders and the Boers were irreconcilable. The former demanded citizenship rights; the latter foresaw that they could be swamped by alien immigrants if they granted the demand.

In London in that summer of 1899 the prospect of another war with the Boers was very much in the air, but the Government was reluctant to send substantial reinforcements to South Africa for fear of exacerbating an already delicate situation and appearing in the role of big bully in the eyes of world opinion. In September, however, belated authority was given for the despatch of British forces totalling about 10,000 men from home, the Mediterranean area and India.

These troops were the first to be involved in what became the largest movement of forces overseas that any contry had ever undertaken. Plenty of shipping was available and overseas commitments and wars were nothing new, but what was new in South Africa in the last three months of 1899 was the critical time factor. From Southampton to the Cape was a three weeks' passage; to Durban a week more. Fortunately about half the September reinforcements were stationed in India, destined for Natal, and most took the relatively short sea passage – 15 to 17 days – from Bombay to Durban, where the first unit landed on 2 October. It was none too soon.

On 9 October the Transvaal Government issued an ultimatum with a time limit of two days. Britain was required to withdraw troops from the borders of the Transvaal, remove from South Africa all reinforcements landed since the previous June, and refrain from landing those then on their way from overseas. The ultimatum was rejected, and on 12 October the forces of the Transvaal and the Orange Free State jointly invaded Natal.

Detailed plans for the despatch of a British Field Force to South Africa in the event of war had been ready since June, and when war came mobilization went smoothly. Sixty-six ships conveyed the Expeditionary Force the 6,000 miles from Britain to the Cape, continuing the shuttle service which had begun ferrying the earlier batch of reinforcements from home in the last week of September.

Meanwhile British forces on the ground in South Africa in the critical early weeks of the war were inferior in numbers and fire-power to the Boers. When war broke out, British forces in Natal totalled less than 16,000 men. The Transvaal Burgher Army alone totalled nearly 27,000 men.

Within 48 hours of the outbreak of war, two large modern cruisers of the Royal Navy arrived at the Cape from opposite ends of the world, carrying men and guns destined to play a significant role in the first six months of the war. They were HMS *Terrible*, on passage from Portsmouth to the Far East, and her sister-ship HMS *Powerful*, homeward bound from the China station, commanded respectively by Captains Percy Scott and the Hon. Hedworth Lambton.

The cruisers were due to exchange stations and had been re-routed via the Cape because of the political situation there. It was a wise decision on the part of the Admiralty, though when their Lordships issued the orders three weeks earlier, they did not know just how timely the arrival of the cruisers and, in particular, of Percy Scott, would prove to be.

Percy Scott was the Navy's leading gunnery expert. He had a genius for improvisation and was a thorn in the side of the Whitehall bureaucrats, whom he bombarded with suggestions for improvements in gun-aiming and signalling. His most remarkable exploit up to that time had taken place in Alexandria in 1882 during the anti-foreign riots instigated

3

by Arabi Pasha. At the time the British Army held a suburb of the town, but were outgunned by rebel forces. Scott, then a Lieutenant, took three 7-inch, 7-ton guns from a deserted fort and had them dragged into a position commanding the rebel lines by means of a block and tackle and the combined efforts of 1,000 men and two railway locomotives!

On taking over command of HMS *Terrible* in September 1899, Scott found much to criticize in the ship's armament. In his autobiography he wrote:

'At this time, when no interest was taken in ships hitting the target or not, the appliances for laying the guns were deplorably bad. The guns themselves were good, and the authorities seemed to think that the matter ended there, and that the gun-sight, which is the all-important element in hitting, was of no consequence.

'From the fighting point of view, I made an inspection of HMS *Terrible* on leaving England, and found that the gun-sights of the 9.2-inch guns were wrongly constructed and unserviceable; that the gun-sights of the 6-inch guns were unserviceable, as they could not be adjusted with sufficient accuracy; and that as for the bow guns put in for firing when chasing the enemy, the object of pursuit would be invisible through the sight, as the port was not large enough, and the guns could not be loaded for want of room to open the breech. These defects applied not to HMS *Terrible* alone, but to every ship.

'If we met an enemy I wanted to have a chance, so the only thing to do was to alter these ridiculous contrivances supplied by the Admiralty as best we could. The low-power telescopes we replaced by others of high power, and we made the cross-wires by making free with the head of a midshipman who had marvellously fine hair.'

And so, luckily for the British Empire, the Navy's leading Do-It-Yourself expert steamed into Simonstown on 14 October for a rendezvous with Hedworth Lambton – another independent-minded officer – and HMS *Powerful*. And Scott wasn't waiting for orders from anyone.

'After being 24 hours at the Cape, I realised the seriousness of the situation. We had insufficient troops to resist the Boer inva-

4

sion; our base was 6,000 miles from the scene of operations, and we had no artillery to cope with the enemy's, either in power or range. It was the experience of the Crimea and the Indian Mutiny and Egypt over again.

'We had on board long-range 12-pounder guns, specially supplied for use against torpedo boats. They were superior in range to any field artillery that either we or the Boers had in the field. It occurred to me that there would be no difficulty in mounting these guns on wheels for service on shore. I purchased a pair of Cape waggon wheels and an axle-tree, and made a sketch embodying my rough ideas.

'Mr Johns, our excellent carpenter, remained up all night with some of his shipwrights and blacksmiths hard at work, and in 24 hours we had this little gun ready. To make sure that everything was right, we fired a few rounds, and the mounting behaved very well.'

On 20 October, before these guns were ready for use on land, a Naval brigade, drawn from the two cruisers and two other warships on the Cape station, and equipped with conventional field artillery only, was landed to guard an important railway junction where a Boer attack was expected. It was the first of several brigades from HM ships which were to serve ashore alongside the Army.

On 25 October the Naval Commander-in-Chief at Simonstown received a telegram from Lieut.-General Sir George White, commanding forces in Natal, asking for Naval personnel and long-range naval guns to be sent to reinforce his artillery in Ladysmith. While HMS *Powerful* stood by at Simonstown ready to leave for Durban in answer to General White's appeal, Scott improvised land mounts for two heavy 4.7-inch guns. These, together with the long-range 12-pounders already adapted for land use, were loaded on board Lambton's cruiser which then made for Durban at full speed. The brigade disembarked and travelled overnight by rail to Ladysmith. On arrival they found a battle in progress. They immediately went into action alongside the Army and succeeded in silencing a long-range gun which was bombarding the town.

5

The battle was fought on 30 October. It had taken the Navy just six days to adapt the guns, transport them 1,000 miles and engage the enemy.

These guns undoubtedly saved Ladysmith. They could have hit the besieging Boers even harder if the Brigade had been allowed to take sufficient ammunition with them, but although Scott asked permission to send 5,000 rounds with the 4.7-inch guns, he was allowed to send only 500, about enough for 25 minutes of quick firing by both guns together.

Lambton scrounged two more 12-pounder guns in Durban, but the Senior Naval Officer there got into such hot water with his C-in-C at Simonstown for allowing this to happen that he was forbidden to let Lambton have any more ammunition. By the time the Admiral relented – he was not prepared to denude the ships under his command of guns or ammunition for land use, though there was no other potentially hostile naval force within 6,000 miles – it was too late; the Boers had cut the railway line to Ladysmith.

CHAPTER TWO

Rendezvous in Ladysmith

I THE NAVAL BRIGADE

CHARLES REYNOLDS SHARP was born on 20 March 1883, one of five children of Charles Seward Sharp, chief cashier of Barclays Bank, Lombard Street, in the City of London. At the age of nine he went to Magdalen College School as a chorister.

When he reached the age of 14 he wanted to be a Naval officer, so the question of getting a cadetship arose. In those days it was necessary to pull a few strings, and my grandfather enlisted the help of a relative, John Talbot, Member of Parliament for Oxford University, who put in a good word with the First Lord of the Admiralty, Mr Edward Goschen.

Reynolds Sharp's name was duly placed on the First Lord's private list of nominations for a cadetship, but my grandfather was notified that 'in the event of a change of administration' the application would have to be renewed. Fortunately, Lord Salisbury's Unionist Government remained in power and in 1898 Reynolds Sharp joined HMS *Britannia* at Dartmouth.

In those days, cadets were trained in sail and lived on board the old wooden warship moored in the river Dart. Sharp found life in HMS *Britannia* very much to his liking. 'We were fed and looked after properly, and I was extremely interested in the subjects taught', he told me. 'In fact I could hardly keep away from my work. I used to carry my books ashore and read them under the trees to master them as best I could.'

The boy's enthusiasm was reflected in his reports, and at the beginning of his last term his case was again raised with

7

Mr Goschen. 'May I venture,' wrote my grandfather, 'to put before you the boy's ambition for the next step in his career. If at the convenience of the Service, and it is considered suitable, he could be sent to the Flagship or other vessel on the China Station, it would be to his great delight, and possibly make him keener in the good work, I gather from his reports, he is doing.'

I have no record of the official reply my grandfather received, but in August 1899 Cadet Sharp passed out from HMS *Britannia* in eighth place out of a class of 60, with 100% marks in practical navigation, charts and instruments, and top marks in seamanship. Only his French let him down: 81 out of a possible 250. He never could master the language!

Early in September it seemed that my father's ambition was to be realised. In the new edition of the Navy List his name appeared on the strength of the cruiser *Orlando*, then on the China Station. He received orders from the Commanding Officer of HMS *Terrible* at Portsmouth to report for passage to the Far East. What followed turned out to be the experience of a lifetime – but in South Africa, and all before his seventeenth birthday. Here is his own account.

'I was very lucky. After passing out from the *Britannia* I was appointed to my first seagoing ship, the *Terrible* at Portsmouth. She sailed for the Far East on 19 September 1899, and in addition to her crew of about 750, carried about 700 supernumerares for the various ships in the China station. We had 30 ships out there then: England was a great country! Our relief was our sister-ship the *Powerful*, which left Hong Kong on 17 September with a lot of men for home, so they were overmanned too. Not only that, but the captain, Hedworth Lambton, called at Mauritius and picked up half a battalion of the King's Own Yorkshire Light Infantry, who were very badly needed at the Cape. There were no orders to shift them, mind you, but Lambton was the man to step into the breach when it was obviously indicated. That was before the days of wireless, and *Terrible's* first port of call was at Plymouth, on 20 September, to pick up the latest orders. We were told to go straight out to the Cape of Good Hope and rendezvous with our opposite number from China at Simonstown, instead of going via the Suez Canal.

'In those days ships all burned coal, and our next call after Plymouth was at Las Palmas, which was an Admiralty coaling station. Those ships ate coal and we put in nearly 2,000 tons and got in a most frightful mess! The officers couldn't be distinguished from the men, in fact I got a good kick in the stomach and was told to get away from someone else's hoist. When the man who had kicked me saw who I was, he was most apologetic!

'Afterwards there was always the business of getting clean. I sent my servant, who was a bandsman, down below to get my tin case, and lo and behold, it came up with a whole side strained open. All my white clothes had gone which I was going to assume the next day, because we were getting into a hot climate. That was a horrible blow to me, as we had got all these things ready for China. So I had to borrow and luckily a kind brother midshipman fixed me up. On leaving South Africa some months later to go home they told me that the clothes had been found. One of the bandsmen was the culprit, and they had left him behind on the breakwater in Durban, breaking stones.

'My ship called at St Helena on the way to the Cape and we were given leave to visit Napoleon's tomb, which I found very interesting. After we had left St Helena, I was on the morning watch one day. My officer of the watch was Lieut. Bogle, a fellow who was always up to some mischief or other. "Sharp", he said, "go down and tell the master-at-Arms (George Crowe) I want to see him." This was about 4.30 in the morning, so down I went from the tremendously high bridge – ladder after ladder – to fetch the Master-at-Arms. Up he comes with me, then Bogle said: "Master-at-Arms, I want to tell you we've sighted a ship homeward bound who has made a signal" – this was with a wink – "to say that war had been declared in South Africa. I thought it might interest the ship's company." So of course down went the Master-at-Arms and put it round the ship's company. There were 1,500 men on board and there was great rejoicing at the thought of a bit of a scrap, which sounds terrible – but it's true. And when we arrived at Simonstown, sure enough, the war had actually broken out a day or so before.

'Our relief, the *Powerful*, had arrived there a day ahead of us.

There was a South African squadron in those days and the Admiral, Sir Robert Hastings Harris, lived there in a house on the beach, and very nice too!

'The captains of the two cruisers, Percy Scott and Hedworth Lambton, were invited to dinner with the Admiral one evening, and I had the privilege of taking Percy Scott in and bringing him off again in the ship's gig. That same night the Admiral had a telegram from Sir George White, who was in Ladysmith with several thousand troops, landed mostly from India, asking for help with guns. He found that his artillery was outranged by the Boers, who had bought one or two very long range guns from Creusot in France. The 15-pounder field gun which our Army had in those days had no range at all. Now Sir George had been a subaltern during the Indian Mutiny, when a Naval Brigade had helped the Army, and this is where he got the idea of using Naval guns in South Africa.

'Those two cruisers, *Terrible* and *Powerful*, were the biggest cruisers we had at the time and between them they carried over 100 guns. *Terrible* had about sixteen 6-inch guns and a lot of smaller ones.

'Percy Scott got to work in the dockyard adapting some of our guns for use on land. I remember seeing him go down the gangway when I was lying in because I had been up late the night before. He produced some guns on improvised mountings which were highly successful.

'On the 26th I transferred to *Powerful* and we sailed for Durban the same day, carrying some guns fitted with Percy Scott's land mounts. We arrived at Durban on the 29th, disembarked and left for Ladysmith in two special trains. Ours was the last train to get in before the Boers cut the line. The last train the other way carried General French, commanding cavalry in Natal, and his A.D.C. Douglas Haig.

'Our brigade consisted of Captain Hedworth Lambton, four lieutenants, a paymaster, a surgeon, two engineers, a gunner, seven midshipmen of whom I was the junior, and 266 men.

'In Ladysmith we had very little equipment in the way of clothes, and various things that soldiers bring out from England. They had wonderful arrangements made by the Army & Navy Stores who provided them with every sort of convenience for camping. We had nothing, and the soldiers up there were very kind

10

to us and said: "Come on, what can we do for you? Will you have a drink?" Well, after a little while there was nothing to drink. "We're sorry we've nothing to drink, would you like a bath?" – and so on. They made us very comfortable indeed. I remember the Gordon Highlanders were our particular friends.

'While our brigade from *Powerful* was doing its stuff inside Ladysmith, *Terrible* came up to Durban and Percy Scott was appointed Commandant of the place. He spent the time preparing to repel the Boer, who was expected to by-pass Ladysmith, which luckily never happened. He improved on the mountings of those guns he had made in Simonstown, and managed to mount a 6-inch gun on wheels, which was a great feat because the gun itself weighs five tons, let alone the mounting.

'After it was all over there was some criticism thrown at us about our poor shooting in Ladysmith. The critics didn't understand that a gun designed to operate at sea level would behave quite differently at high altitude, and we were over 3,000 feet up in Ladysmith. Today of course they would have it all worked out so that you could adjust the sights according to the altitude; but there was nothing like that in 1899.'

Reynolds Sharp was the youngest officer in Ladysmith, but only by two months. Edward Chichester, born in January 1883, had also transferred from *Terrible* to *Powerful* at short notice, and was now one of the Ladysmith Brigade's seven midshipmen. Chichester had also joined *Terrible* for passage to China, embarking at Devonport. His father, Captain Sir Edward Chichester, R.N., 9th Baronet, was appointed Principal Transport Officer in South Africa on the outbreak of war, responsible for disembarkation of the thousands of troops who eventually arrived. So young Edward started pulling a few strings as soon as he got to the Cape. A letter to his mother tells the story.

'*HMS Terrible, Simonstown, Sunday 22 October 1899*.

'I have lots of news for you this mail, so here goes for a chat. You must have been surprised when the news of war came out, and so were we when we came in here. The signal flying from the flagship (*Doris*) read: "Boers declared war two days ago." Any amount has happened since then and everyone is extremely excited. I

11

immediately sent off a wire to Dad who replied soon after saying he had requested the Admiral to appoint me to the Naval brigade. But I was not among the list, sad to say, as they appointed them by seniority and there are three above me who haven't been appointed. I have just had a wire from Dad to say he is coming down to the Cape tomorrow, so I shall find out all about it then. I am dining with the Admiral tonight so I shall find out why he has not done what he was asked to do by the Governor.

'Our Marines have gone to the front, and we cheered them when they left the ship. We are anxiously awaiting orders to land field guns and battalions.

'Latest news says Boers defeated in two glorious battles but about a dozen officers and 60 men of ours killed. General Symons they say is mortally wounded and yesterday we were told by wire he was dead. But this morning the rumour is contradicted by the Admiral.

'Yesterday I biked to Capetown, 25 miles. It was a lovely road for about 20 miles across open veldt and under mountains, but the last 5 miles were frightfully bad. All of us went up to the range the other day for rifle shooting, and we had great fun up there. First of all we had to walk up a great mountain, then across the veldt for about a mile to the range. We saw a couple of eagles right up at the top of one of the mountains. We bought eggs from Boer farmers and boiled them over a fire in a biscuit tin. After we had finished the firing we went snake-hunting, as there were supposed to be any amount of puff-adders and other snakes about. However we only saw one which was a grass-snake and about 3 ft. long which we killed.

'There is a gale of wind on in this place which makes going and coming off from shore very nasty. I hope we land a naval battalion as we shall get a medal then, but I do not think we shall otherwise.

'I suppose you are back at Youlston now again. If we have luck we shall return to England after the war with troops or invalids or something of the sort, in which case a little leave will come in. Otherwise we shall have to go straight on to China.

'I have found my helmet and bedding. They were stored away in the Marines' storeroom by the Captain of Marines directly they came on board from the *Magnificent*. I am putting any amount of sketches and things in my log now and it is beginning to look quite smart.

'Have you been getting a good many pheasants lately, and have Uncle Charles, etc. had good sport? I suppose Aunty Fan is still up at Youlston with you? I must write to her also. It is now Tuesday and as the mail goes tomorrow I must finish off my letter. The Boers are now massing outside Kimberley, about 10,000 of them.

'Well, I dined with the Admiral on Tuesday night (24 October). Captain Percy Scott was there. He said that Dad was most anxious I should go to the front, if there was a chance.

'You can see the mountains 40 miles across the bay here, and they are a very fine sight. I am afraid I am not telling you much news in this letter as I fancy I have gone off letter-writing lately. I have lost my pipe, worse luck, the one G.B. gave me. I am sending you some silver leaves which I got myself and they can only be got here so mind you keep them. I will try and get you some decent ones.

'Please tell Aunty Fan I am awfully sorry but I am sure that she would not relish a letter from me this week as I have not got anything decent to say to her. But I will write to her *honestly* next week when I will try to save up some news.'

Young Edward Chichester was soon to have plenty of news for his family. His only problem was getting it out of Ladysmith.

II THE GORDON HIGHLANDERS

As Reynolds Sharp has said, a close relationship was established between the Naval Brigade in Ladysmith and the Gordon Highlanders. The regiment's 2nd Battalion had been part of the reinforcements sent from India to South Africa before war broke out. The battalion's Transport Officer was Lieut. Ian Forbes.

Ian Rose Innes Foster Forbes was born at Jacobabad in Sind Province (now in Pakistan) on 25 October 1875, the second son of Colonel John Forbes of Rothiemay, Banffshire, who was in the Indian Cavalry. He was educated at Blair Lodge School, Polmont and went into the Gordon Highlanders in 1894 through the Militia. He joined the Regiment's 2nd Bn in 1896 and went to India in 1898.

There were plenty of distractions available to officers

stationed near the foothills of the Himalayas in the summer of 1899, but the references to polo, duck shooting and whist in Forbes's diary came to an abrupt end on 8 September, when an urgent wire was received:

'Regiment ordered to South Africa for active service: concentrate Umballa'.

The battalion left Umballa (Ambala, in the modern transliteration) on 18 September and endured a tedious rail journey to Bombay where they embarked on two transports for the passage to Durban, arriving on the day of the Boer ultimatum. Forbes's main responsibility on the voyage was for the welfare of the battalion's 108 mules.

Of the arrival at Durban, Forbes wrote: 'Crowds and great reception. Presentation of an address. Left for Lady-smith by the last train at 5.30 with the mules and 64 men. Refreshments all along the line.'

The battalion arrived at Ladysmith the next day.

'We have tin huts to live in,' he wrote. 'No bed or anything. This place is a very desolate spot, nothing but dust. Very cold at night; about 4,000 feet up.'

On 11 October Forbes wrote of 'great rumours of war. Outposts out all day and night, also patrols.'

The next day was an 'awful day of rain. Very busy sending out supplies to the picket. Got very wet. At 3.00 got the order to prepare to move at any moment, so changed and got the mules ready. War declared by the Transvaal and Orange Free State Republics against Great Britain. Great joy and excitement.'

There was no immediate threat to Ladysmith, and for the next few days the Gordons were out on exercises and settling in generally, the weather at the time being hot and dusty by day and cold at night.

On the 18th the permanent 'tin' camp, which was in an exposed position, was evacuated and the regiment moved to another site under canvas. Forbes described the new camp as 'very comfortable indeed', but went on: 'Began to rain and thunder at 7.00 and went on all night. Tents all flooded.'

III   THE GARRISON COMMANDER

At the time of his appointment to the Natal command, Lieut.-General Sir George White was Quartermaster-General at the War Office and due to go to Gibraltar as Governor. The Boer War caused his appointment to the Rock to be deferred for nearly a year.

George Stuart White was born on 6 July, 1835 at Portstewart, Co. Londonderry, one of nine children of James White. He was educated at King William's College, Isle of Man and Sandhurst. In 1853 he was gazetted an Ensign in the 27th Inniskillings. The following year his regiment was ordered to India and was there when the Mutiny broke out in 1857. The Inniskillings did not see action against the mutineers, being mainly engaged in guarding communications in the Punjab and 'showing the flag.'

After ten years with the Inniskillings, George White transferred to the 92nd Gordon Highlanders, with whom he was to distinguish himself in the field. He took part in the Afghan War of 1879-80 and won the VC at Charasia. In the mid-1880s he was in command in Burma, in the 90s Commander-in-Chief in India – and during this period he became honorary Colonel-in-Chief of his Regiment.

A few days after being appointed to command the Natal Field Force, Sir George White sailed from Southampton in the RMS *Tantallon Castle* and reached Capetown on 3 October 1899. There he had discussions with Sir Alfred Milner and General Forestier-Walker, the local military commander.

It was agreed that the situation in Natal was the most dangerous, and Sir George then continued on his way by train to the port of East London. On the way he read up as much as he could about Natal, and the frequent halts on the line gave him the opportunity of observing the attitudes of the populace of Cape Colony.

15

He took ship again at East London for Durban, and during the passage wrote the first of a series of letters to Lady White which form a diary of the events of the following four months.

'October 6th, 1899, on board SS Scot:
'At nearly every railway station the people appear to be divided into two camps, one English and one Dutch. At some stations the Dutch are leaving our Colony carrying firearms, presumably to join their countrymen across the border. I had not before realised what a large proportion of Dutch there are in the Cape Colony and how sharp-edged is the antagonism between the races. I more than ever now feel how remiss the Government at home have been in not letting military preparation keep pace with political negotiation. For the next three months the Dutch have the best of us as regards armed strength and position. A little success might give them enormous advantages. If the operations go against us in the early part the Cabinet will only have themselves to thank if they have to reconquer South Africa from the sea.'

Sir George reached Durban on 7 October where he was met by Major General Sir W. Penn Symons, from whom he was to take over command. Penn Symons had come to Natal the previous April from the Ambala Command in India, where he had gained a reputation as an officer of great energy.

Penn Symons reported that the troops were stationed at seven different places ranging from the capital, Pietermaritzburg, to Glencoe in the north. This meant that they were dispersed along 160 miles of narrow-gauge, single-track railway. The main base, Ladysmith, lay 120 miles beyond Pietermaritzburg and 40 miles short of Glencoe. The movement of troops from Ladysmith to Glencoe had been ordered by the Governor of the Colony, Sir Walter Hely-Hutchinson, a fortnight previously with the primary object, as he himself recorded, of safeguarding the coal supply from nearby Dundee, which was important both for the railway itself, and for the marine coaling station at Durban.

16

Before leaving London Sir George had had no briefing whatever on the defence plans for the colony and no instructions as to how he should operate. It was perhaps just as well to leave it to the men on the spot, yet the defence of Natal was a highly contentious matter. There was strong political pressure for the defence of the whole colony. On 25 May Sir Alfred Milner had promised that if Natal were attacked, it would be defended 'by the whole force of the Empire.' Two months later the Natal ministers had demanded that steps be taken to defend the whole colony in the light of this pledge.

From a military point of view, however, the northern part of the colony was extremely difficult to defend, even with adequate forces – and these did not start to arrive until six months after Milner's pledge! The terrain favoured the Boers, and the Colony tapered to a point inserted like a wedge between the Orange Free State in the north-west and the Transvaal to the north and east. The Boers from both Republics were known to be concentrating along the frontiers.

This was the dilemma facing Sir George White when he set foot in Natal for the first time. His view was that forces should be concentrated at their main base, Ladysmith, not dispersed, as he now found them. Penn Symons, on the other hand, was the man on the spot; and he was confident of being able to hold his own against the Boers at Dundee.

After his meeting with Penn Symons at Durban, White went on to Pietermaritzburg where on the evening of 9 October, the day of the Boer Ultimatum, he had an interview with the Governor. It was a fateful discussion.

'*11 October, Pietermaritzburg.*

'I am off today to Ladysmith to take command there, where the storm will probably first burst. It is a time of great anxiety, as the Boers' declaration of war comes on us before the arrival of reinforcements that I had hoped to have at my disposal. These include the King's Dragoon Guards, the Gloucesters, the Border Regiment and the Royal Irish Fusiliers, four regiments in all and such a force makes a great difference. I would gladly have the force concentrated at Ladysmith under these circumstances, but I found a force at Glencoe Junction. The Governor of Natal considers that to remove that force now and to concentrate all at Ladysmith would involve a very grave risk of the Natives rising and the Dutchmen in our territory declaring for the enemy.

'Under these conditions I have considered myself bound to fight it out at Ladysmith and at Glencoe. By the time this reaches you I hope the worst will be over, but I cannot hide from myself that we have to face greatly superior numbers in positions in which it is very difficult for us to know where to strike next, or indeed where the enemy may make an effort. They are all round us.

'All along I have considered that more troops should have been poured into South Africa before negotiations proceeded to such extremes.

'I must now shut this up. I feel we may be isolated in a day or two.'

Sir George's premonition was to be fulfilled all too soon. He had disliked having his meagre forces dispersed for political reasons, and it seems that Lord Lansdowne at the War Office shared this view, for he telegraphed:

'Please understand that we expect you to act strictly in accordance with military requirements of the situation. Governor is within his rights in directing your attention to political consequences of your arrangements, but responsibility for the arrangements rests entirely with you. You may find steps necessary which may run counter to public opinion here and in the Colony, but we shall unhesitatingly support you in adhering to arrangements which seem to you, from military point of view, sound.'

Unfortunately this telegram was not sent till 26 October. By then Glencoe had been lost to the enemy. However, the telegram doubtless strengthened White's resolve to adhere to his plan of holding Ladysmith at all costs.

CHAPTER THREE

Natal Invaded

THE Boer commandos from both Republics mounted a
concerted invasion of Natal, crossing the border at six different points. In accordance with the agreed British defence
plan, no attempt was made to hold the extreme north of the
colony, which was occupied by the enemy without resistance. Two of the six Boer commandos – those of Erasmus
and Lukas Meyer – converged on the Glencoe-Dundee area.
On the night of 19-20 October, Meyer's force occupied
Talana and Lennox Hills, overlooking Dundee town and
coalfields, near where General Penn Symons was encamped
with his brigade of 4,000 men. These hills were the scene of
the first battle of the war.

Meyer's force was driven off the hills after a day of fighting, but the British mounted force detailed to cut off the Boer
retreat was itself cut off, and surrendered.

General Symons was among the casualties at Talana,
mortally wounded as he urged his men forward in an
exposed position. The command devolved on General Yule.

So the British won the day, but Meyer got away. Erasmus
had not even been involved, and was encamped only three
miles to the north-west of Dundee. Nor was that all. Koch
had already cut cummunications midway between Glencoe
and Ladysmith by his advance from the north on
Elandslaagte, the scene of the next day's battle, in which the
Boer commandant was opposed by forces sent out from
Ladysmith.

Five companies of the Gordons were called out from the
town to take part in this battle, which was fought on a plain
surrounded on three sides by a horse-shoe shaped ridge, the

Boer laager being on the eastern end of the ridge. Forbes was there:

'We advanced and took up a position on the crest of the hill to the right rear of the guns and opened fire with long range volleys, the Boers returning it with great accuracy and rapidity. Their bullets went high and over the regiment and on to me who was to bring up the ammunition. I had to cross a space of 300 yards or so under a perfect hail of bullets, one striking and grazing my wrist. A carrier was struck just beside me. I had the greatest difficulty in getting the ammunition across owing to the heavy fire and want of men to carry the heavy boxes. All this time we were firing from the crest, the artillery duel going on.'

The decisive stage of the engagement took place just before dusk, during a thunderstorm. The Gordons had worked their way round the Boer flank and were attacking uphill.

'The advance from here to the Boer position was across very stony ground and exposed. The enemy's fire was very accurate and very well kept up. The regiment lost very heavily crossing this ground. We were in line and advanced by rushes. Men were falling very fast indeed. The bottom of the hill was reached leaving a number of them. The regiment then charged the position by a series of rushes, the pipers playing "Highland Laddie", the buglers sounding the charge and the men cheering and shouting "Majuba!"

'The fight ceased in the dark at 7.15 pm. It was raining hard most of the time. Then I lost the regiment, it being pitch dark. I found the Devons and then a Boer wagon with hospital comforts. I went out with whisky and blankets and looked for the wounded. We were out from 8 till 12 midnight and tended nearly 100 of all ranks. A farm house was made into a hospital. There were an awful lot of wounded. It was ghastly work. I made some soup at the farm and went out to the regiment on picquet on top of the last hill. We had 72 prisoners and 100 horses captured. I took off the coats from the killed and put them on the wounded and gave them water-bottles. I then tried to sleep but the cold and wet were too awful. I never spent such a miserable night lying on rocks and mud. It blew a cold wind and rained most of the night.

20

'A Boer prisoner when interviewed said:
' "We came out thinking we should sit down and shoot red-coated English soldiers but we were surprised to see them clothed in invisible kharki." He spoke with bated breath of the Gordons saying their dash, courage and onslaught was too awful and was quite impossible to resist.

'Our men who stayed out with the wounded were very good giving up most of their clothes and sitting in the rain beside them. The wounded with a few exceptions stayed out all night and were brought in in the morning. A burying party was sent out when we got back to camp but were unable to bury the dead as the Boers had reoccupied the position.'

So that battle, too, had been won, but the Boers were still there, blocking General Yule's communications with Ladysmith. The victor of Talana found himself cut off, and was obliged to withdraw by a circuitous route. The retreat, carried out in appalling weather and through a sea of mud, took five days.

While General Yule was withdrawing, the Free State commandos – which had moved into Natal unopposed – occupied hills about eight miles north-east of Ladysmith, from where they threatened the general's line of retreat. On 24 October Sir George White led a force out from Ladysmith and engaged the Freestaters near Rietfontein farm until news came that General Yule's force was safely back in Ladysmith.

'Three Battles. Boers defeated. Symons killed,' was the message one British ship spelled out to another in the South Atlantic shortly after the events just described. The signal caused much elation among the passengers who were on their way to the Cape; but it gave a totally false impression of the situation. Talana and Elandslaagte had indeed been British victories; Rietfontein had been a successful holding action; and General Yule was back. But the Boers, thanks to their superior mobility – they were all mounted – now not only held virtually the whole of Natal north of Ladysmith, but were closing in on the town from all sides.

21

In the hope of breaking the ring, Sir George White sent out a force on 30 October to engage the enemy near Lombard's Kop, about four miles to the north-east. In order to block one of the enemy's possible escape routes to the north of Ladysmith, a force of about 1,000 men under Lieut.-Colonel Carleton moved out under cover of night towards a hill pass called Nicholson's Nek. But everything went wrong for them. They started out late, lost their ammunition, failed to reach their objective, alerted the Boers; and were surrounded on a hilltop. Most of those not killed or wounded surrendered.

Meanwhile, news reached Ladysmith of a possible attack by the Freestaters from the west. Sir George White therefore ordered the force engaged in the Lombard's Kop area to withdraw to the town. The movement was carried out under heavy artillery bombardment. At the same time the town was being shelled by a siege gun from one of the nearby hills, and there was no gun in Ladysmith of sufficient range to reply to it. At this moment in the engagement that became known as the Battle of Ladysmith, the Naval Brigade for which Sir George White had telegraphed, arrived on the scene. One historian describes the event as a providential diversion. It was certainly the only bright feature of that Mournful Monday.

The British were in fact extremely lucky that the enemy did not press them harder during their withdrawal to Ladysmith, which they could easily have done. Some indication of the conditions of the retreat is given by Ian Forbes in a reference to another regiment:

'They were ordered to retire and they ran back an awful rabble leaving their guns, arms, ammunition and nothing stopped them till they came into camp. It was awful.'

On the Tuesday after Mournful Monday there was an armistice for the exchange of wounded. Forbes wrote:

'No firing, both sides being very busy indeed with getting up their guns. The Boers seem to be very busy and closing round everywhere.'

By Thursday, 2 November, the Boers completed the encirclement of the town, cutting the telegraph link with the south – and the water supply. The siege that was to last for four months and share the world's headlines with Kimberley and Mafeking, had begun.

CHAPTER FOUR
The Siege and the Relief Campaign

OF the three Boer War sieges, Ladysmith has not rated very highly with historians. It was the shortest; there was no newsworthy clash of personalities, as occurred between Cecil Rhodes and the Garrison Commander in Kimberley; Sir George White did not have the same flair for publicity as Baden-Powell in Mafeking; and there were periods when nothing of any importance happened for days on end.

But the conquest of Natal was the Boers' first priority. Both sides saw Ladysmith as the key to the colony. For the Boers, the capture of Ladysmith was to be the signal for a revolt of their sympathisers, of whom there were many in Cape Colony, throughout British territory.

If the Boers had achieved their aims it would then, as Sir George White put it, have been necessary to reconquer Natal from the sea.

Another feature of Ladysmith which set it apart from the other sieges was that both garrison and civilians suffered considerable hardship during the last two months – January and February, 1900. Food and ammunition were short, water was bad, forage for animals had run out and disease was rife. All this, and a midday temperature round 100°.

But for the skilful husbanding of food supplies and the ability of the Naval guns to hit back (though with strictly rationed ammunition), Ladysmith might indeed have been forced to surrender.

At the turn of the century the town looked like a movie set for a Western. The main street was wide enough for a mule team to make a U-turn; the houses had the authentic wooden façades and corrugated iron roofs. The appearance of the

24

town gave no clue to its significance, which was to be found on flat land two miles from the market square: the 'tin town', a recently-built Army barracks. Ladysmith had become a garrison town, locally known as the 'Aldershot of South Africa.'

Named after the wife of a former Governor of Cape Province, Sir Harry Smith, the town owed its importance to the railway. The narrow-gauge line from Durban divided there, one branch continuing to the Transvaal, the other to Harrismith in the Orange Free State.

As the *Times* correspondent of the day aptly described it, the town lies in the bend of a horseshoe, but the hills which make this formation are disconnected and the ranges and spurs straggle over a large area. Defence of the town was rendered difficult by an outer ring of hills, higher than the horseshoe ridge in the town, and outside the perimeter held by the garrison. There was insufficient manpower for the defence of these outer hills, and in Boer hands they were a natural choice for siege gun-emplacements – and the Boers had been buying just the right sort of guns for this purpose.

The defenders were thus at a disadvantage from the start. The garrison numbered 12,500 officers and men. Civilians totalled 5,400, plus about 2,400 Kaffirs and Indians, making a total ration strength of about 21,300. Food supplies at normal consumption rates were sufficient for two months. There were nearly 10,000 horses and mules and 2,500 oxen, but forage supplies for one month only.

One consequence of the siege was the immobilization of almost the entire Natal Field Force, leaving the Colony virtually defenceless until the Expeditionary Force started arriving from England at the end of November. Fortunately for Britain, the Boers were too cautious after their success in investing Ladysmith to risk a large-scale invasion of Southern Natal. Only a small Boer force penetrated some 50 miles further into the Colony, crossing the Tugela river in the process. This river zig-zags in a roughly easterly direction about 12 to 15 miles south of Ladysmith.

The country between Ladysmith and the Tugela is hilly and strongly favoured the Boer defence in the campaign for the relief of the town which was fought in that area from the end of November, 1899.

Neither side expected the siege to last for more than a few weeks. The British knew that help was on its way. The relief column, when it assembled at the end of November, was only 25 miles away from the town.

For their part, the Boers expected the British to surrender after a few weeks' bombardment at most. Had not the British surrendered at Potchefstroom and Majuba in the First Boer War 18 years earlier?

Both combatants fought according to a code of chivalry which belongs to a bygone age, when prisoners of war and enemy wounded were treated, if anything, better than one's own casualties.

It was a kind of siege that the world will certainly never witness again.

The Boer recipe for success at Ladysmith was patience, vigilance and bombardment – bombardment by the latest in French and German heavy ordnance, far outranging the Royal Artillery's guns.

The first Creusot 155-mm gun started firing from Bulwana Hill early in the morning of 2 November and continued throughout the day, causing considerable alarm among the civilian population. Many took refuge during daylight hours in caves beside the Klip river which flows through the town. Some of the garrison's defensive positions were exposed to bombardment; the units involved, including the Gordons, had a very uncomfortable time and were obliged to dig holes in which to take refuge.

Initially, all shops closed and business was suspended, but within a few days they reopened and carried on until their stocks were exhausted.

However, the timing of the bombardment was usually predictable, with breaks for meals and seldom any firing after dark or, in accordance with Boer religious principles,

26

on Sundays. The shells caused surprisingly little damage and relatively few casualties, though there were occasions when a single shell claimed a number of victims.

One reason for the ineffectiveness of the bombardment was that it was not properly co-ordinated; another, that the guns were outside shrapnel range and the common shells were mostly either blind or smothered in soft ground. The camp of one Royal Field Artillery Brigade was exposed to daily shelling; it contained 600 men, the same number of horses, yet in four months the only casualties in camp were four men wounded and one horse and six mules killed.

On the second day of the siege an incident took place which was characteristic of the attitude of the Boers to war. The Creusot gun on Bulwana Hill which was bombarding the town at a range beyond that of all except the British Naval guns, developed a fault and was dismantled. While they tackled repairs, the Boers hoisted a flag of truce. The British thereupon ceased fire until the Boer gun was operational again!

The outer ring of hills surrounding the town, on which the Boers placed their heavy guns, provided natural grandstands from which to observe the bombardment, and were so used on occasions by the Boer womenfolk.

On 3 November the garrison made its first sortie towards enemy positions. A reconnaissance went out to Lancer's Hill to the south-west under General Brocklehurst, commanding cavalry. It met with strong opposition from the Heilbron burghers. Total British casualties were five killed, one missing and 28 wounded.

There was an armistice on 4 November, when Sir George White asked Commandant-General Joubert for permission to evacuate all civilians and sick personnel to Southern Natal. Joubert refused this request, but permitted a neutral camp to be established at Intombi, three miles south of Ladysmith on the railway to Colenso and Durban. A train was allowed to operate a once daily shuttle service between the town and the camp.

27

The first Sunday of the siege set the pattern for the rest of the period: a day of rest for the gunners. The following Monday was also a quiet day. The Naval brigade were engaged in mounting a 4.7-inch gun on 'Cove Redoubt', a hill in the northern defences, and christened it 'Lady Anne' after a relative of Captain Lambton, the second 4.7-inch gun was nicknamed 'Bloody Mary' by the bluejackets. A control post or 'conning tower' for the Naval guns was then established and connected by field telephone to the batteries, and Sir George White's headquarters were also linked into the network. A similar system was used in Kimberley and Mafeking. It was the world debut of the field telephone in war.

On 9 November the Boers attacked. A general bombardment started at 5 am to which the Naval guns immediately replied. One hour later, the squadron of the 5th Lancers (dismounted) on Observation Hill came under heavy fire from the Pretoria burghers advancing on the town's northern defences from the direction of Bell's Kopje. The Lancers were reinforced by two companies of the Rifle Brigade from Leicester Post, and the enemy was driven back. Meanwhile the Vryheid burghers attacked the Platrand – Caesar's Camp, to the British – the plateau forming the town's southern defence line. Captain Macready of the Gordons described the hill as follows:

'Caesar's Camp is a long flat-topped hill, the sides to the south and west, in the direction of the enemy, being precipitous boulder-covered slopes clothed in a tangled mass of trees and undergrowth, the northern end terminating in a small round-topped eminence which went by the name of Wagon Hill. From the inner crest of this plateau the enemy would have been able to overlook and dominate with fire the whole of the defences of Ladysmith.'

On this occasion the Boer attack was beaten back by the Manchesters and the 42nd battery RFA, supported by the Imperial Light Horse, but in the new year the same area was to be the scene of the only major battle of the siege.

By midday on 9 November it was obvious that the situation was under control, and as it was the Prince of Wales's birthday, a salute of 21 guns was fired, with shotted charge. The Naval 4.7-inch guns fired the first and last shots.

Later in the day, Boers opposite Helpmakaar Hill made a demonstration against the Devons and the Liverpools. The total British casualties of the day were four killed and 27 wounded. The Boers were reported to have fired over 850 shells.

The next ten days were wet and misty, and bombardment was suspended in consequence. On the 12th the Boers asked the British ambulance camp for some chlorodyne to treat the dysentery from which both sides were suffering. They got some, and some brandy as well.

On 13 November the garrison carried out a reconnaissance to Star Kopje to ascertain the Boer strength on that hill.

On the night of 23-24 November the garrison made an ingenious but unsuccessful attempt to block the railway leading to the Orange Free State frontier. When a train was seen to arrive at the Boer railhead, the British sent an empty locomotive fitted with explosive charges on the buffers along the line in the hope that it would collide with the train, but it ran off the line at a curve and did no damage.

Later the same day the garrison suffered a severe loss of trek oxen. A herd which was grazing under the supervision of Kaffirs, strayed towards the Boer lines. The Leicesters tried to head them back but the Boers, by aiming their shells to fall just beyond them succeeded in driving 228 head into their own lines, only 30 or 40 being recovered by the garrison. The result was an immediate reduction in the British meat ration.

Meanwhile since the middle of the month the first transports bringing the Expeditionary Force from England had begun to reach the Cape and Durban. General Sir Redvers Buller, V.C., the Commander-in-Chief, arrived at the Cape on 31 October and immediately found it necessary to revise

29

the original plan of campaign. This had envisaged a northward push from Cape Province on Bloemfontein and a subsequent further advance into the Transvaal. The initial Boer
successes in Natal which had taken place while Buller was on
the high seas forced him to divert to Natal some units originally intended for use in Cape Colony. Buller decided to take
personal command of the Ladysmith Relief Column, with
Lieut.-General Sir C.F. Clery, Commander of the 2nd Division, as his Second-in-Command. Throughout the vicis-
situdes of the Ladysmith relief campaign – and these were to
be many – Buller remained in personal command in Natal.

Buller reached Durban on 25 November, only a few days
after the arrival of the first units of the Expeditionary Force
and on 6 December set up his headquarters at Frere, 25 miles
from Ladysmith. Meanwhile the Boer raiding columns,
which at one stage had penetrated as far as the Mooi river, 25
miles beyond Frere towards Pietermaritzburg, retired back
across the Tugela River.

Within a few days of the establishment of Buller's Frere
H.Q. a well-equipped force was available there. It included
a Naval Brigade, commanded by Captain E.P. Jones, HMS
Forte, composed of detachments from *Terrible*, *Forte* and *Tar-
tar*. To it were attached the Natal Naval Volunteers. Its
armament consisted of two 4.7-inch and fourteen 12-
pounder long-range guns.

At the end of November another Boer 6-inch gun started
bombarding Ladysmith from Middle Hill, near Wagon Hill
on the southern perimeter of the defences. The garrison
moved two howitzers up within range of the gun under cover
of darkness and silenced it on 30 November, killing or
wounding nine gunners. The Boer gun reappeared 12 days
later on Telegraph Hill to the north of the town, a suitable
event for inclusion in a news-sheet entitled 'Ladysmith
Lyre', full of the latest 'shaves', the jargon of the day for
unconfirmed military reports or 'tall stories,' and first produced by the journalists in Ladysmith a fortnight before.
The first issue of this publication, written by the joint efforts

of the journalists in the town, started with a "Prospectus".

The *Ladysmith Lyre*, they wrote, "is published to supply a long felt want. What you want in a besieged town, cut off from the world, is news which you can absolutely rely on as false. The rumours that pass from tongue to tongue may, for all we know, be occasionally true. Our news we guarantee to be false. In the collection and preparation of falsehoods we shall spare to effort and no expense. It is enough for us that Ladysmith wants stories; it shall have them."

The town hall, used as a hospital and flying the Red Cross flag, was shelled on 30 November, ten men being killed and others severely wounded. Apparently the Boers assumed that the British must be using the building for some warlike purpose, as they already had a hospital outside at Intombi. As a result of the shelling, the town hospital was moved to a ravine out of the line of fire. The area chosen was most insalubrious, being subject to violent dust-storms.

In preparation for a junction with General Clery's force, Sir George White had given orders on 2 November for a mobile column of all arms to be kept permanently ready to move at half an hour's notice, carrying three days' rations.

On the night of 7-8 December a sortie was carried out under General Sir A. Hunter, Chief of Staff, against Boer heavy guns on Gun Hill to the east of the town. It achieved complete surprise, and the guns were destroyed at the cost of one officer and seven men wounded.

The following day two companies of the 1st Liverpools accompanied by a squadron of the 19th Hussars, attacked and captured Limit Hill. The Hussars went beyond the hill to destroy the telegraph lines and burn many shelters occupied by the enemy.

A reconnaissance was also sent out along the road towards the Transvaal. It met with heavy rifle and gunfire and was forced back with the loss of three men killed and three officers and 18 men wounded. This action caused the Boers to transfer 2,000 men back to Ladysmith from the Tugela front.

On the night of 10-11 December a sortie was carried out to Surprise Hill, to destroy a 4.7-inch enemy howitzer. Unfortunately the first charge placed in the gun failed to explode. By the time the gun had been successfully destroyed the enemy had been alerted and the attackers suffered 64 casualties, including 26 killed or missing.

During the first month of the siege carrier pigeons were the only reliable means of getting messages out of the town. Photographic copies of maps for the use of the relief column were also sent out by pigeon. At that time only the immediate Ladysmith area had been properly surveyed, and the maps did not extend as far as the Tugela river, one of the main obstacles in Buller's relief campaign.

The officer who prepared the Ladysmith maps shortly before the war, had been inhibited by lack of adequate funds and the overriding need to avoid arousing Boer suspicions as to his motives. No proper maps existed for other areas of Natal – or for the Orange Free State and Cape Colony either – and Buller had to rely on rough maps of local farms, without contours, and often inaccurate in such detail as they showed.

Special maps were produced for the British Official History of the war and they are a gift to the armchair strategist armed with hindsight. And today, the picture changes yet again, for the industrial development of Natal involves the damming of the Tugela basin and consequent transformation of the countryside.

Captain Percy Scott devised a method of signalling by morse code with a searchlight and Venetian blind shutter – the forerunner of the Aldis lamp. A complete outfit was mounted on a railway truck and sent up the line towards the Tugela front. The lamp was aimed at the clouds at night so as to 'bounce' signals into Ladysmith.

From December two-way heliograph signalling was established between Ladysmith and a hill near Weenen, 35 miles to the south east.

Native runners also carried messages in and out of the

town, and were much used by the journalists, but often intercepted by the Boers.

From Buller's headquarters at Frere the direct route to Ladysmith lay along the road and railway which crossed the river at the village of Colenso. But the Boers held commanding positions on hills on both sides of the river in that area. In view of this, Buller's initial plan was to cross the Tugela 16 miles further west at Potgieters Drift from where, in spite of the considerable detour, he judged the approach to Ladysmith to be easier.

Buller had informed Sir George White of his intention to attempt a crossing at Potgieters Drift on 17 December and it was envisaged that the mobile column held ready in Ladysmith would go out to effect a junction with the relief column.

However, news came in at this juncture of reverses sustained in two other battle areas, those at Stormberg railway junction in Cape Colony on 10 December and Magersfontein near Kimberley the following day. In the light of these developments Buller decided against the detour to Potgieters Drift and in favour of a direct attack in the Colenso area. With reason, he wished to avoid lengthening his lines of communication and the possibility of himself being cut off like Sir George White.

Buller communicated his change of plan to Sir George White, but then brought forward the attack to 15 December without telling him. On that date his artillery opened up. The guns were only 12 to 15 miles from Ladysmith and clearly audible in the besieged town. As far as anyone in Ladysmith knew, it could have been the preliminary bombardment to the attack as originally scheduled for two days later.

On the 16th, a heliogram to Ladysmith revealed what had happened: Buller had attacked at Colenso, and had failed. An attempted frontal assault on the Boer positions on the north bank of the Tugela had been repulsed, and the losses told their own story: British casualties were 1,139, the Boers lost 6 killed, one drowned and 22 wounded.

33

Friday's failure at Colenso, following the previous Sunday's defeat at Magersfontein and Monday's at Stormberg, made up the 'Black Week', which marked the nadir of British fortunes and morale.

Buller was much criticised at the time – and later – for his handling of the whole campaign. It is only fair to add that the Boers were also dissatisfied with the outcome at Colenso. They were lying low in concealed positions hoping to lure the British across the river and annihilate them. The plan misfired because the Boers gave away their positions by opening fire prematurely. The British were operating on relatively flat land on the right (south) bank of the river, and their every move was observed by the Boers on the high ground beyond the river and on Hlangwane Hill, on the British side of the river and to the east of Colenso.

More remarkable than the military reverse of Colenso was the effect of the battle on Buller's morale, and the exchanges with Ladysmith and Whitehall which resulted. His heliogram to Sir George White reporting his failure went on to suggest that, as he (Buller) could not attack again for at least a month, Sir George should consider firing off his ammunition, burning secret papers and making the best terms he could with the enemy. Sir George endeavoured to persuade Buller not to lose heart and assured him that he (White) had provisions for six weeks and no intention of surrendering.

When repeated to London, Buller's 'surrender' telegram elicited the following answer from Lord Lansdowne, Secretary of State for War:

'Her Majesty's Government regard the abandonment and consequent surrender of White's force as a national disaster of the greatest magnitude.'

The cabinet thereupon appointed Field-Marshal Lord Roberts to succeed Buller and General Lord Kitchener to be his Chief of Staff. Roberts's appointment was made in such haste that there was no prior consultation with the Commander-in-Chief Lord Wolseley.

Roberts sailed for South Africa a few days later, his ship called at Gibraltar to pick up Kitchener who had arrived there from Egypt, and they reached the Cape on 10 January 1900. They then took over the conduct of the war from Buller, but left him in charge in Natal.

The news of Buller's reverse was released to the Ladysmith garrison, though not the 'surrender' proposal. There was little activity in the town at the time, the principal matters of concern being the large number of fever cases, with a total of nearly 2,000 patients in the Intombi hospital; the high price of food; and the impending exhaustion of supplies of forage for animals.

On Christmas Day the garrison organized a sports meeting including an inter-service tug of war and mule races. A Christmas party for the 250 children was organized by Colonel Frank Rhodes (whose brother Cecil was in Kimberley) and Major Davis of the Imperial Light Horse. With the thermometer registering 103° in the shade, Father Christmas appeared in traditional garb and distributed presents, and though rations were running low the garrison got their turkey and plum pudding, but no liquor. Queen Victoria telegraphed to Sir George White:

'I wish you all my brave soldiers and sailors a Merry Christmas. May God guard and protect you.'

The Boers fired a shell into the town which failed to explode and buried itself in the ground. When dug out it proved to be full of Christmas pudding and had inscribed on it the flags of the South African Republics and the motto: 'With the compliments of the season.'

The year ended with fever cases still on the increase (they reached their peak at the end of January), forage exhausted, cattle for slaughter finished (trek ox on the ration) and still no early prospect of relief.

By this time the shortage of ammunition for the Naval guns had become serious. Only a limited quantity had been

35

brought into the town and on 27 December Ian Forbes noted that there were only 181 rounds left for the two 4.7-inch guns. The need to conserve ammunition against an emergency – such as was to occur on 6 January 1900 – prevented effective reply to bombardment by the Boers, and in the new year one of the guns was silent for one whole month for lack of ammunition.

The garrison commander also had less serious matters to consider, including a petition from the Town Council asking that soldiers be forbidden to bathe in the river as the ladies liked walking along the banks, and could not do so as the soldiers were naked!

On 5 January, 1900 Commandant-General Joubert held a Boer Council of War at which it was decided to attack the southern defences of the town. Each Republic contributed 2,000 men, reinforced by 600 burghers withdrawn from the commandos facing Buller along the Tugela front. Both contingents left their laagers at midnight on 5-6 January.

The same evening a party of British sappers had been working on emplacements for Naval guns on Wagon Hill. One of the guns, a 4.7-inch, had been moved from Junction Hill in the town's northern defences, and was left in its wagon at the foot of the hill pending completion of the emplacement. A patrol had gone out towards Middle Hill and returned at about 2 am, reporting that all was quiet.

The Boers attacked at 2.40 am and there followed 17 hours of fighting, ending in complete victory for the defenders, whose first-hand accounts of the battle are given in the next chapter.

British casualties on 6 January were: 14 officers, 135 NCOs and men killed; 3 officers and men died of wounds; 28 officers, 221 NCOs and men wounded, totalling 424. Boer casualties were 184 killed and 380 wounded.

It was a particularly sad day for the Gordons, as amongst those killed was their Commanding Officer Lieut.-Colonel W.H. Dick-Cunyngham, V.C. He was bringing up his regiment to the attack when he was hit by a stray bullet and died later of peritonitis. Only a short time previously he had returned to duty after recovering from wounds suffered at Elandslaagte.

In the meantime Buller had reverted to his original plan of taking the indirect route to Ladysmith. With the arrival of another division commanded by General Sir Charles Warren, his force now numbered 30,000 men. There then followed a further seven weeks of campaigning before the final breakthrough to Ladysmith. The intervals between the various actions were caused by the slow rate of movement of the forces and their supplies, the excessive size of the supply train and the lack of a local water supply. Mules and oxen were the principal motive power, the average speed of an ox team being one mile per hour. The progress of the campaign can be summarised as follows:

17 January :	Crossing of the Tugela at Trickhardt's Drift.
16-24 January :	British losses 1,750; Boers about 400.
23-27 January :	Capture and subsequent abandonment of Spion Kop.
5- 7 February :	Abortive attempt at breakthrough via Vaal Krantz.
17-18 February :	Return to Colenso area for successful advance on Ladysmith.

During this agonising period of waiting while listening to British gunfire that was never more than 16 miles distant, both garrison and civilians in Ladysmith were getting weaker and fever claimed more and more victims. By the middle of January only 9,500 of the original 13,500 men of the garrison were fit for duty, coal supplies needed to operate the condensers producing drinking water, had been exhausted and light-hearted sports meetings were a thing of the past. Yet the defences of the town were further strengthened, especially the Caesar's Camp plateau.

On 24 January hopes of relief were again raised in vain by the distant sound and – for those with a naval telescope on Caesar's Camp – view of the battle of Spion Kop. Three days later fever cases at Intombi hospital reached their peak at 1,314. As the month ended the average of deaths was eight per day and 1,100 horses, for which no more forage was available, were turned loose to graze as best they could.

In February horses were slaughtered in large numbers for food, and 'Chevril' horse extract was produced for human consumption. The daily bread ration varied between ½-lb and 1-lb per person. By this time the garrison no longer had the strength to make a sortie or demonstration to assist Buller's force.

Relief finally came after 119 days, on 28 February.

Following this outline of the siege and the campaign for the relief of the town, it is time to let those who were actually in Ladysmith tell their own story.

CHAPTER FIVE
Inside Ladysmith

EDITOR'S NOTE

This chapter is mainly composed of extracts from Reynolds Sharp's log and Ian Forbes's diary; from Sir George White's letters to Lady White; and Edward Chichester's letters to his father.

I have also included some despatches of three journalists who went through the siege: H.W. Nevinson of the *Daily Chronicle*, H.H.S. Pearse of the *Daily News* and G.W. Steevens of the *Daily Mail*. Steevens died of enteric fever in January, 1900.

Additional details of the Boer attack of 6 January 1900 have been taken from Colonel M. Jacson's History of the Devonshire Regiment and Major John Selby's 'The Boer War'. A brief linking narrative has been added to bring the events of this day into perspective.

The source is given at the beginning of each section or paragraph.

Cross-headings have been inserted where the text is not self-explanatory, and notes will be found at the end of the chapter.

29 October 1899

SHARP: 10.30 am came into Durban in 10 3/4 fathoms; hands employed hoisting out 4.7-in guns, 12-pr guns, ammunition, Maxims, stores and kits. 5.00 pm landed first half of Naval brigade. We got straight from the tugs into the train. Started about 8 pm, arrived at Maritzburg about 12.30 am, got through to Ladysmith by about 9.30 the next morning.

30 October

Arrived this morning at Ladysmith about 9.30 am after a very tedious night journey. Three 6-in shells passed just over our heads and burst about 100 yards beyond the station as we were untraining the guns. The three 12-prs were lim-

bered up behind bullock-waggons and sent straight out to
the front where a battle was in progress with 'B' Co as a gun
guard. We marched along the Newcastle road until we got to
Limit Hill where we found the Devons entrenched. Just as
we were about to unlimber and open fire, we received orders
to retire with all possible speed. We returned as fast as we
were able but the bullocks were very slow. One ammunition
waggon galloped in, the others followed quickly. All along
the road were ambulance waggons, each of which was going
as fast as it could. This made our progress still slower. The
6-in gun on Pepworth then opened fire on us. The first shell
hit an ambulance waggon, the second burst just under the
wheels of our first 12-pr, overturned it and wounded all the
gun's crew, Emly seriously, Ford and Nail slightly. The
bullocks bolted and left the gun. Lieut. Heneage dismantled it
and brought in the striker. The next shell burst about 20 yards
to our right, and the next hit some medical officers. We retired
to the plain between Observation Hill and Junction Hill and
opened fire at 6,500 yards and silenced the gun. After this an
armistice was declared to bury the dead and collect the wounded. We took over 12-prs on Gordon Post where we found the
Natal Naval Volunteers with a 3-pr Hotchkiss. We entrenched
the 12-prs and Maxims here and pitched our tents after dark in
rear of the guns.

31 October

We opened fire early. They returned, putting three or four
shells into our camp and five or six into the cavalry. We had
no fortifications at all and it was very lucky no one was hit.
An armistice all day. Employed getting up stores, ammunition, etc., from the station and strengthening gun pits, sangars and so on. We have now pitched our camp just over the
rise which covers us from 'Long Tom', the Boer 6-in gun on
Pepworth Hill.

1 November

FORBES: Very wet night. Awful discomfort for those without

40

tents. Up at 7.30. No firing, both sides being very busy indeed with getting up their guns. We had breakfast à la câfé style in the open. Then I went up to the post and had a look around. The Boers seem to be very busy and closing round everywhere. At 10.30 the order came to shift camp and we are now in the camp vacated by the Irish Fusiliers, down by the iron bridge – a good camp but not so interesting, being away from the gun posts but safer.

CHICHESTER: You will have seen now or heard, I daresay, that I am up here attached to Powerful's Naval Brigade. We arrived here on Monday morning (30 October) having arrived at Durban on Sunday at about 11 am. By 6 pm we were all on board a train bound for Ladysmith with two 4.7 in, three 12-prs (12 cwt), one 12-pr (8 cwt) and three Maxims.

We were received very cordially all the way up the line, stopping at two stations for half an hour for hot coffee. At 6 am Monday morning we arrived at Ladysmith and immediately we fell in on the platform. Three minutes after, a shell came clean over us and soon after three more from 'Long Thomas', a 6-inch gun of the enemy's mounted 8,000 yards or thereabouts from the camp. We then advanced to within 3 miles of the enemy with our field guns to a kopje on gaining which we were ordered to retire as a general retirement was going on all round. We did so under a heavy fire from Long Thomas, one shell dismounting one of our guns, the last one, and wounding three of the crew in the head. We had to leave the gun, but afterwards re-took it, righted it and brought it back to camp. I believe the Rifles suffered pretty heavily while doing so.

We have been shelled continually by Long Thomas, which from a projectile which was found not burst today turns out to be a 6-in with a much shorter projectile than what we use. Now they have got three positions and we are being shelled pretty heavily from front and both flanks.

I am going to send this probably by one of the Natal Naval

41

Volunteers, an officer servant named Velcoup and a reliable man. He lives in Durban and I expect you will be there, at least hope not at Capetown. A lot of men, ours too, have gone down with dysentery, which is a bad look-out.

The Captain, the Hon. Hedworth Lambton, is awfully decent and very popular. It is going to rain tonight, worse luck. It is rather rot sleeping on the side of a hill with only a waterproof sheet over you.

2 November

SHARP: Manned the guns at 4 am. The 4.7-in gun on Junction Hill is now ready and the Captain went over there to fire. A scaling charge was first fired; we then opened fire on Long Tom on Pepworth who returned our fire. The 4.7 was firing about three shots to his one, and every time he fired, our 12-prs on Gordon Post fired simultaneously. The mounting of the 4.7 lifted slightly after the first few shots. We soon got their range and made excellent shooting. Their shells were pitching all round our gun; one passed through the top of the earthworks and severely wounded Lieut. Egerton who was in command of the gun, passing through both legs. We ceased firing after about 40 rounds had been fired. In the afternoon the 4.7 was under a very hot fire from five guns, one 6-in, two 12-prs, two 7-prs, of the mountain battery. Lieut. Hodges is now in command. Communication was completely cut off and the town is closely invested. Poor Lieut. Egerton died this evening; everybody feels his loss very much.

3 November

Manned the trenches as usual at 3.45 am. At 8 am the Boers opened fire with 6-in and 12-prs, we returned with a few rounds from the 4.7 and 12-prs. During the afternoon we have a very good shot with the 4.7-in, they then waved a white flag; we ceased firing; about half an hour later they fired again but it fell very wide.

5 November

STEEVENS: The Boer gunners seldom began before breakfast; knocked off regularly for meals – the luncheon interval was 11.30 to 12 for riflemen and 12 to 12.30 for gunners; hardly ever fired after tea-time, and never when it rained.

THE NAVAL BRIGADE'S 'CONNING TOWER'
6 November

We come to what looks like a sandbag redoubt, but in the eyes of heaven it is a conning tower. On either side, from behind the sandbag epaulement, a 12-pr and a Maxim thrust forth vigilant eyes. The sandbag plating of the conning tower was six feet thick and shoulder-high; the rivets were red earth, loose but binding; on the parapets sprouted tufts of grass, unabashed and rejoicing in the summer weather. Against the parapet leaned a couple of men with the clean-cut, clean-shaven jaw and chin of the Naval officer, and half-a-dozen bearded bluejackets. They stared hard out of sun-puckered eyes over the billows of kopje and veldt. Forward we look down on the one 4.7 in, aft we look up to the other. On bow and beam and quarter we look out on the enemy's fleet. Deserted Pepworth is on the port bow, Gun Hill under Lombard's Kop to starboard, Bulwan abeam, Middle Hill astern, Surprise Hill on the port quarter.

8 November

FORBES: We were shelled out of our camp at 10.30 am till 12.30. Wrote letters as I am writing this in my hole. In the afternoon rode with Baird up to Junction Hill and photoed the big gun. When the enemy fire we fire immediately on seeing the smoke and our shell reaches them 3 seconds before theirs reaches us. Musketry fire goes on practically all day, chiefly by the enemy at long ranges from 1,000 yards. The way the enemy get their big guns up hills is this: They knock the ends out of a strong barrel and place the gun in it fixed as an axle, then 37 teams – 370 oxen – drag it up the hill.

43

9 November

Wakened at 5.00 am by the bombardment commencing. The fire was very heavy indeed, all the guns in the place seem to have been at it at first. We all fled into our holes and were confined therein from 6.00 till 1 pm. Several shells fell very close to, and one among the cooks knocking them down without injury. At 12.30 the fire slackened. In the afternoon our gun planted lyddite shells near Long James. Two attacks were made and went on all day, one on Caesar's Camp and one on the North Side, both repelled with losses, the Manchesters, Leicesters, Rifle Brigade and the 60th being the troops employed.

SHARP: At 12 noon fired a salute of 21 guns with shell in honour of the Prince of Wales's Birthday. The Boers returned with 9 guns, also with shell. A little more rifle fire later, and a few shots from Long Tom, one of which blew up the gunroom sucking pig during the afternoon.

NEVINSON: What should we have done without the Naval guns? We have nothing else but ordinary field artillery, quite unable to reply to the heavy guns which the Boers have now placed round the town.

RECONNAISSANCE TO STAR KOPJE TO ASCERTAIN BOER STRENGTH

13 November

STEEVENS: Our guns fired at the Boer guns until they were silent; then the Boer dismounted men fired at our dismounted men; then we came home. We had one wounded, but they say they discovered the Boer strength on the Kopje, outside Range Post, to be 500 or 600. I doubt if it is as much, but in any case two men and a boy could have found out all that three batteries and three regiments did.

FORBES: It is reported a carriage and pair and an escort of 50 men brought a man supposed to be Kruger to a farm hard by. Yesterday an Irishman came in and said there were 25,000 Boers round the town and they were confident of getting in. They believed that 2,700 men were killed on Thursday (9 November) and that we are now only 2,000 strong.

15 November

At 12.30 am awakened by an awful row, all the Boer guns went off at once and shells came flying round everywhere. Everyone got up and went to their holes. I went back to bed and slept till 6.

16 November

Three Middies came down to us and had a bath and wash not having had one for over four weeks. Madame Joubert drove up to see the big gun at Pepworth. After firing two shots at it, it being supposed to have been removed, it replied nearly killing the staff and killing two men and wounding five. We expect to be here for five or eight weeks more.

SHARP: When we manned the trenches in the morning Masters, A.B., vaulted over the parapet and sat on his own bayonet. Luckily he did not hurt himself seriously although the bayonet went in right up to the hilt. The sick orderly on being asked by the M.O. replied: 'Bayonet passed through the port cheek of his backside.'

18 November

FORBES: At the start of a football match a shell came from Long Tom and went through a tent with four men in it and burst just between two tents without doing any damage.

20 November

At 9.30 pm the enemy turned on a searchlight and kept it on me for a long time. A very awful position to be in. Sent out patrols in two hour reliefs. At 12.00 all the guns opened fire; five shells came to us but seemed to do no damage.

21 November

SHARP: Frightfully hot day. Colonel Knox just put up a dummy battery on the plain facing Bulwana. The Boers wasted a lot of ammunition on it.

22 November

FORBES: We are covering all our white tents with mud and making them all kharki colour. The system of firing by the Boers is that each gun in turn fires so many rounds and so on all round. The enemy signalled to Maiden Castle: 'You must all be getting fat' – 'where is the balloon?'

228 HEAD OF OXEN LOST TO BOERS

24 November

NEVINSON: Who knows whether by Christmas we shall not be glad of even a bit of trek ox?

25 November

FORBES: In the afternoon played whist and at 5 had awful fun with the mule gymkhana. First event was tentpegging with swords.

26 November

The Navy are putting a gun on Caesar's Camp and we supplied two companies as escort and the working party to dig the hole for it. Our chaplain in his prayer said: 'Guide the shells into waste places' and at that moment a shell landed in the scrub hard by.

NEVINSON: The pathetic gratitude with which the first issue of the 'Ladysmith Lyre' was received proves that to appreciate literature of the highest order, you only have to be shut up for a month under shell-fire.

27 November

SHARP: The Boers opened fire at about 8.30 am with all their guns which now amount to three 6-in, three 4.7-in howitzers and a whole host of 15-prs and 12-prs, pompoms, Maxims, etc. The new gun which we have mounted on Caesar's Camp with Midshipman Carnegie in charge, replied to the enemy fire.

NEVINSON: The great event of the day was the firing of the new 'Long Tom.' The Boers placed it yesterday on Middle Hill, the hill beyond Wagon Hill, where the 60th hold our extreme post towards the West. It is a 6-in Creusot. He did about £5 damage at the cost of £200.

'I wish to heaven the relief column would hurry up', sighed a young officer to me. 'Poor fellow', I thought, 'he longs for the letters from his own true love.' 'You see, we can't get any more Quaker Oats,' the young officer explained.

CONDITIONS IN THE EMERGENCY TOWN HOSPITAL

NEVINSON: The sand and dust and dry filth, gathered up by the hot west wind from the plain of the old camp, swept in a continuous yellow cloud along the road and down the ravine. It blotted out the sun, it blinded horses and men, it covered the wounded with a thick layer. Imagine what it is like to extract bullets, to staunch blood, to amputate.

FORBES: Several thousand Boers were seen coming from Colenso to Middle Hill. It seems from information gained that General Clery with 18,000 men is advancing here. The informant, a kaffir, says there are 'plenty too much Englishmen' coming. Firing was heard to the south yesterday so we may be relieved soon.

28 November

A shell took the head off a saddler sergeant of Hussars and he went galloping on, a ghastly sight.

29 November

SHARP: At about 2.30 am there was very heavy rifle fire in front of Observation Hill. We opened fire about 5 am and

47

were answered from all sides. It appears that there was to have been an attack by two brigades on Rifleman's Ridge this morning but the enemy got wind of this and the order was countermanded at 9 pm. We however were not informed of the cancellation and opened fire.

FORBES: When ordering his bluejackets to advance to repel an enemy attack, Captain Lambton said: 'Go at the double but only doing knees up and gaining little ground so that the enemy thinks you are advancing very fast and will thus fire across your bows.'

1 December

When the sentries hear a shell coming they immediately stand at ease quite smartly and correctly. Pepworth Tom has had his nose blown off. The gun on Gun Hill is new and shoots horribly straight. Communication was established with Weenen Hill 35 miles away but none of the signals received has been published.

2 December

After dinner walked up to the chemist's in town and when there was ordered to double back. The regiment turned out in 35 minutes complete in every way and went to the rendezvous. The whole of the troops turned out, orders being to operate towards Limit Hill. Back at 12.00 as it was only a ruse or a rehearsal. We were there one hour before anybody else arrived.

RETURN TO DUTY OF LT.-COL. W.H. DICK-CUNYNGHAM, V.C.
WOUNDED AT ELANDSLAAGTE

3 December

The Colonel came into camp. The pipers played him in and the whole regiment turned out and cheered him. Went up to lunch and tea with the Middies. Last night a man was caught signalling to Bulwana. Another man yesterday, a driver of the Imperial Light Horse, was caught signalling to the enemy where their shots were falling.

Two more companies, E and F, went up to the bottom of Caesar's Camp called officially 'Fly Kraal.'

4 December

Papers say that Ladysmith would fall on November 24. White went out walking in plain clothes without a pass and was captured and taken up to Bethune's picquet for identification. Fifteen thousand men have got to Estcourt and Colenso and relief will come within 14 days.

5 December

Intended playing polo but it first rained shells then water so I put it off.

6 December

PEARSE: The daily bombardment is now so much a matter of course that one hardly makes a note of it unless some casualty brings home the fact to us that nobody is safe while shells fly about. During a heavy cannonade in which our Naval batteries engaged Gun Hill and Bulwana from 6.00 am to 10.00 am women and children were walking about the street quite unconcerned.

Our losses since the siege began 36 days ago are 13 killed and 148 wounded.

7 December

FORBES: Old Anderson the QMS was walking along when a shell came and nearly took his head off. He afterwards remarked: 'I had to bob but I should'na hae bobbed.'

8 December

At 10 pm on Thursday 7 December, 500 men of the Natal Carbineers and 100 men of the Imperial Light Horse went out with two guides, natives of the place, to capture the guns on Gun Hill. A small party of Engineers with guncotton etc., went with them. They were all dismounted and marched out to the end of Helpmakaar Hill, turned to the left and advanced up the Hill. A party of the Natal Carbineers went to the right to protect them from troops coming to the assistance of those on Gun Hill. When they got half-way up the hill they were challenged from the left rear and someone answered them in Dutch but an ass of a man chaffed about it in English so the Boer sentry loosed off his piece and dashed up the hill. General Hunter who led the force then said: 'Fix bayonets' which was rather odd for they had none to fix. The men rattled their carbines against the stones to sound like fixing bayonets and they all dashed on shouting 'Cold Steel' to deceive the Boers. At this the crowd on the top fled and the hill was taken. Cordons were made round the guns and the engineers placed their charges. There were three guns: a 6-in breech-loading gun, a 4.7-in howitzer and a .308 Maxim machine gun. Two charges of guncotton were placed in the big gun which had its muzzle blown off and body bulged. The breech and block were brought away by the I.L.H.

8 December

SHARP: The following is an extract from a letter found on Gun Hill, translated from the Dutch:

'Dear Sister, it is a month and 7 days since we besieged Ladysmith and we don't know what will happen further. The English we see every day walking about the town and we are bombarding the town every day with our cannons. They have erected plenty of breastworks outside the town and it is very dangerous to attack it. Near the town are two naval guns from which we receive very heavy fire which we cannot stand. I think there will be much blood shed before they surrender, as Mr Englishman fights hard and well. Our Burghers are a bit frightened.'

9 December

Had very bad news today about the poor Commander's death at Graspan, also Huddart, Midshipman from the *Doris*. The Naval brigade there did very well and were complimented by Lord Methuen.

CHICHESTER: How are you? Hope you are all well. I think there will be a chance of sending this down on Tuesday, or thereabouts as the relief column is expected then.

Well, any amount of things have happened since the line was cut. They have four 6-in guns up here blazing away at us besides two 4.5-in howitzers and about six 12-prs with innumerable smaller weapons. One 6-in on Pepworth Hill called 'Long Tom', we are supposed to have knocked out about a week ago. Another 6-in, however, was put up on Gun Hill, part of Lombard's Kop, soon after, and it was conjectured whether it was the same one or not. Then there is another 6-in on Umbulwana called Bulwani or Big Ben; there is also one more 6-in on End Hill which is firing the opposite way to us, probably at the advance guard of the reliefs. This gun was put out of action once by two of our 6.3-in howitzers which get right under the lee of the hill and blaze away and of course cannot be seen by the enemy who always fire over them. The 6-in, though, has been repaired and has shifted to End Hill. Then there is a 4.5-in and 12-pr Pom-pom on Surprise Hill on our left flank which eventually after blazing bang in the middle of our camp every night at 12 pm or thereabouts made us shift quarters. One of them killed the gunroom pig, which was a great loss. So much for the guns; I have left out Silent Susan, a 12-pr about 3,000 yards away which you can't hear go off but only when the shell comes whizzing at you. There is also a gun called Diarrhoea Jack which is a 1¼-lb. Maxim thing and makes a row just like its name.

I hear there is going to be a clasp for Elandslaagte, and one

51

for Ladysmith. They have done little damage in the town (£7,000 estimated). I am now in command of a Company, the Lieutenant being in command of one of the 4.7's and the other Mid in command of a 12-pr on Caesar's Camp. I go out with my Company every other night on picket on Observation Hill, which has to be held at all costs (What Ho!). We shall of course spend Christmas Day here so could you send me up a turkey or plum duff for the gunroom as we can't get anything here beyond rations. Everything is sold out: no jam, milk, butter, cheese or any blooming other thing. Whisky is now 21 shillings a bottle and butter five bob a pound so you can guess the price of things. I suppose you will inform Mother that I am all right, so I will not write to her till after I have heard from you. I wrote her a line, just before leaving the ship. We hear today per runner that the Naval Brigade at Modder River lost 90 killed and wounded, the Commander being one of the first killed. The *Powerful* has now lost her Commander and Gunnery Lieutenant, the two most popular officers in the ship.

I have had a mild form of dysentery the last five days, but am getting better now. On Monday we silenced Long Tom in three rounds but he's at it again continually. One 4.7-in was mounted this morning and has been making some splendid shots, but this gun of the enemy's is protected by any quantity of sandbags and of course presents a very small target. Honestly speaking we are in a tightest corner now, and we are anxiously awaiting the arrival of Buller.

The enemy will *not* advance although they swore they would take Ladysmith yesterday. If they would advance we could lick 'em in the open but the beggars get 5 miles off and pound away with their big guns which seem to be gathering in numbers day by day. There's no doubt that the place would have been in a very bad position if it hadn't been for the arrival of our guns.

SIR GEORGE WHITE: I think I may commence a letter to you as Sir Redvers Buller is approaching the Tugela and we may reasonably expect some hard fighting within the next week, the result of which I hope will be the relief of Ladysmith, and the opening of our communications with the outside world from which we have been so long cut off. I have been in good health all the time but it has been weary work. I fought in the open as long as I could with a superior enemy on both sides of me. I was heartbroken over the loss of the Gloucestershire Regiment, the Royal Irish Fusiliers and the Mountain Battery and of course I now wish with all my heart I had not sent them out, but two regiments and a battery ought to have been able to hold their own against the number of Boers sent against them which, as far as I can make out, were only 750 men.

We occupy a very large position here. It is some 13 miles round. This is rendered necessary by the immense range of the enemy's guns. One big 6-in gun which annoyed us for a very long time threw a shell into our lines to a distance of over 10,000 yards from the gun. When this is repeated north, south, east and west of us, it makes it hot for us but it is remarkable how few casualties there have been. The soldiers spend the days in shelters which save them from the shells. Most of the officers and civil residents have also dug themselves shelters underground. The escapes have been marvellous. I have over and over again seen shells bursting amidst groups of soldiers and horses without hurting anyone.

There are several women and children still in Ladysmith. Thank Goodness none of the children has been hit and only one woman. A 6-in shell burst actually in the room in which this woman was sitting and blew everything to ribbons and the whole side out of the house.

Sometimes the Boer guns bombard us at night and this is distressful. The night before last my Chief of Staff, Major-

General Sir Archibald Hunter led a party of 600 picked men and made a raid on Gun Hill, one of the enemy's positions round Ladysmith. He surprised the post and took three guns including one of the enemy's largest (6-in) guns.

I am so pleased not only because that gun was doing us much harm but also because Hunter is such a delightful fellow and has done so well all through the siege and previous operations. You will like to hear of our mess and manner of life. All the Headquarter Staff live in the same house which we have commandeered. This is the list:

Sir G. White
Col. Duff
Capt. F. Lyon
Capt. Dixon, my Acting ADC
Major-Gen. Sir Archibald Hunter, Chief of Staff
Capt. King, ADC to Gen. Hunter
Col. Ian Hamilton
Lieut.-Col. Sir Henry Rawlinson

We have had plenty to eat and to drink and we keep very early hours. I am up about 4 o'clock every morning and we generally retire between 9 and 10 o'clock. At one time before our defences were as strong as they are now I used always to sleep in my clothes ready to turn out in a second; but now a large proportion of the Boer Army has gone south to face the relieving force on the Tugela and I turn in regularly. Most of the Regimental officers, however, have to sleep in the open with their men in strong points built of stones heaped together. There is no dearth of this class of building material in Natal. The climate is very variable; some days are very hot, about as hot as Simla in mid-June, or perhaps a little hotter. We then have a severe thunderstorm with most vivid lightning and this cools the weather down greatly.

Ladysmith is a nasty place and I fear there will be a terrible plague of enteric if we are kept much longer. Already there are 80 cases and the numbers are increasing rapidly. We had more enteric fever here last year than in any other station of the British Army and I dread the result of siege conditions this year far more than the shells and bullets of the enemy.

We have also a bad prospect of horse sickness which is very bad at Ladysmith and usually sets in about this time. The flies are a terrible nuisance. The number of horses, mules, cattle, etc., bring them in myriads. In our dining room, which is very small, we catch them on fly papers and in wire domes in millions but it does not seem to decrease their numbers. They get into everything left uncovered.

Ian Hamilton has done extremely well in this campaign and is I think sure to get a KGB (and I hope a VC) for which I have recommended him. He was very brave at Elandslaagte and General French who commanded there – I was present but did not assume command – recommended him to me, a recommendation I was of course very glad to support.

I had a bit of a fight with the Boers yesterday. Wishing to take advantage of General Hunter's successful raid on the enemy's guns I made a demonstration with the cavalry to make the enemy believe I intended to attack to the north and make him uneasy about his communications in that direction. The enemy was very quick and the cavalry were not worked quite as I wished, so we had heavier losses than I had anticipated but my object was to make them increase their force north of me and decrease their force which is between me and Sir Redvers. This purpose was effected as at least 1,000 more Boers have moved round.

I have plenty of provisions greatly due to Colonel Ward's foresight and excellent organisation. He is an admirable officer and deserves all that can be bestowed on him for his masterly arrangements. Whatever we want, we go to Ward, and he finds it for us.

11 December

SHARP: The Rifle Brigade under General Howard went out this morning and captured and blew up the 4.7-in howitzer on Surprise Hill. Unfortunately the fuse missed fire at the first time and delayed them about half an hour and they had

55

to fight their way back at the point of the bayonet. In the afternoon a new gun opened fire from Telegraph Hill (or else the Middle Hill gun has been moved).

13 December

Pratt's 12-pr has now gone to join the 4.7-in gun on Wagon Hill. I went to hospital today with dysentery. Archer, A.B., who was wounded in the head, died.

PEARSE: The Devons and Gordons have to lie behind earthworks or in bombproof structures, half tent, half cave, shelled when they venture to move out by day, kept on the alert through many hours of weary night and called to arms again one hour before dawn.

FORBES: A market in the town where eggs were nine shillings and sixpence a dozen, potatoes 48 shillings a small sack. At 8.30 am orders came that we were to go out on flying column scale. The arrangements went off well with the exception of Fly Kraal baggage. Back by about 11 pm. Sickness is increasing: 700 men at Intombi; four funerals and 82 admissions today.

Firing was heard to the south-west.

We escorted two guns (one 4.7-in and one 12-pr) to Caesar's Camp. They were out all night.

THE BATTLE OF COLENSO

15 December

SHARP: The shells fired by the relieving column were plainly seen today. Bulwana fired several rounds, and Telegraph Hill and the howitzers exchanged a good many shots.

15 December

FORBES: Enteric is ravaging the troops. At Intombi there are 2,000 patients in all. We have only three sick men. Prices are up: 13 shillings and sixpence a dozen eggs; potatoes £3 per sack.

WHITE: This is a great Boer fête day, Dingaan's Day, being the name of a Kaffir chief they defeated heavily on this date in 1838. I had hoped that Buller's force would have relieved me by now, but news has come in this morning through the signallers that there has been a fight south of the Tugela, result not yet known. This disappoints me much as I thought Buller's force had driven all the enemy to this side of the river and that he would be here in a few days.

Enteric fever is very bad here and increasing at quite an alarming rate. Three weeks ago we had about 15 cases; today we have 180. Where to place the sick in Ladysmith is a difficulty. The entire town is swept by the enemy's shells and we hid the small hospital in a donga. Our principal hospital is outside Ladysmith and clear of fire under an arrangement made by me with Joubert. Yesterday we had a terrific thunderstorm and the donga was flooded, the hospital with it.

FORBES: The new scheme of defence came out. We are to be in reserve as a whole battalion and to be always ready to move anywhere. In order to carry this out as rapidly as possible 54 wagons have been collected and we had 16 men go in each and then the wagons go at full gallop.

19 December

FORBES: Dull day with rain. The temperature has dropped from 105°F to about 50°F.

NEVINSON: It seems incredible that two British armies should be within 20 miles of each other and powerless to move.

21 December

WHITE: I was lying on my bed not able to raise my head off the pillow when a shell from the big gun on Bulwana hit the house and carried away the room next to mine. Sir Henry Rawlinson had a narrow escape. The shell carried away the chair in which he had been sitting a few minutes before.

Our house was knocked to pieces and we have had to shift the headquarters to another house where I go for meals, but I have taken up my abode at a nice new house on a hill which is exposed to shell fire. So far the Boers have not got information that I am living in it and it is not regularly aimed at. Some of their spies have been asking where I have gone to as they know they knocked my house down.

FORBES: The sickness is increasing: 800-odd ill now and an average of seven funerals a day. We have only six sick out of 812 men.

22 December

PEARSE: This was a day of heavy calamity for one regiment, and marked by more serious casualties than any other since the siege began. At 6 o'clock this morning a shell from Bulwana struck the camp of the ill-fated Gloucesters on Junction Hill just as the men were at breakfast. It killed six and wounded nine, of whom three are very seriously hurt. A little later a shell from the big gun on Telegraph Hill fell into the cavalry lines. It burst among the 5th Lancers who were at morning inspection, and wounded Col. Fawcett, Major King, a Captain, the Adjutant, a senior Lieutenant, the Regimental Sergeant-Major a troop Sergeant-Major and a Sergeant. The last had an eye knocked out, but the others were only slightly wounded, and when their injuries had been looked to, they all formed in a group to be photographed.

NEVINSON: The worst of it all is that we can no longer reply for fear of wasting ammunition.

23 December

SHARP: Midshipman Chichester came out to Intombi today with enteric fever.

PEARSE: We have done our best to endure shells, privations, and the approach of a sickly season with fortitude if not absolute cheerfulness, and our hope is that though the position here may not seem a very glorious one, it will be recognised henceforth as an example of the way in which British soldiers and colonists of British descent can bear themselves in circumstances that try the best qualities of men and women.

'I wonder what they think of us in England now? Do they regard us as heroes or damned fools for stopping here?' asked an officer of the King's Royal Rifles with comic seriousness. This question was heliographed to our comrades south of the Tugela one day, and the answering flashes came back, 'You are heroes; not – – '. Here the message was interrupted by clouds. We flatter ourselves that the missing words were full of generous appreciation.

At Christmas time a Boer was talking under a flag of truce with an English officer about the prospects on each side. 'We admit,' he said, 'the British soldiers are the best in the world, and your regimental officers the bravest, but – we rely on your generals!'

25 December

FORBES: At 4.05 am a tremendous musketry fire started all along Rifleman's Ridge. It lasted for 10 minutes and showed that there were hundreds of Boers on the alert. I think they expected an attack for there was nothing to fire at.

26 December

The heat is too awful: 112°F in the tents. Buller telegraphed to White: 'Hope all is well with you. I am still hopeful of relieving you.' The Boers fired 180 shells, but there were no casualties. In the afternoon a whole crowd of women, perhaps 100, were standing on Bulwana watching the firing.

Our gun 'Bloody Mary' is getting worn out. Six rounds is all that we can fire in a week.

Out of 180 shells fired at us today there were no casualties.

27 December

The following is the amount of ammunition left: for 4.7-in Naval guns 181; 12-pr Naval guns 640; 15-pr field guns 9,600 or 200 per gun. Howitzers 560, small guns 2,600 and the 2 Elandslaagte guns 160.

28 December

Eggs 16 shillings and sixpence a dozen.

A civilian refugee from Johannesburg came and had a talk with me. He took my account of the Elandslaagte battle with him as he is writing a book. There are 1,500 men in hospital.

30 December

Prices of foodstuffs rise daily. 56 lbs of potatoes cost 60 shillings, one bottle of whisky £5, one tin of milk 10 shillings, cigarettes one shilling each.

NEVINSON: Almost the saddest part of the siege is the condition of the animals. The oxen are skeletons of hunger, the few cows hardly give a pint of milk apiece, the horses are failing.

Passing the field hospital I saw stretcher after stretcher moving slowly along in their blankets.

'Dysentery, enteric; enteric, dysentery' were the invariable answers. All the thousands of shells thrown at us in the last two months count for nothing beside the sickness.

SHARP: Heard that Captain Jones is in command of the Naval brigade with Buller.

1 January 1900

PEARSE: As the year ended the rations for humans were holding out well, but forage for horses was getting scarce. 400 men went out daily to cut grass on the hillside least exposed to fire and brought back about 32,000 lbs, but it did not go far.

SHARP: Bulwana and Telegraph Hill started firing early, the howitzers replying to the latter. Lieut. Stabb was taken down to the field hospital today with enteric fever. Heard a little firing down south.

FORBES: Big Ben fired 36 shots which is a record.

In the night we heard the guns at Colenso and flashes were seen, the sound taking 70 seconds to reach us. At 5.00 am the Boer guns opened fire, the first shell falling into the town unfused near the town hall. On it was inscribed: 'With the compliments of the season.' This was sold by the finder for £10. The natives are becoming very frightened and many want to give notice.

2 January

The Hussars were out looting and were bringing in some young pigs. The sailors were lining their parapets and called out: 'The Boers are upon you!' Immediately the Hussars dropped their pigs and bolted; the sailors then went out and collared the lot. Our sick now 1.8%. Cattle are through and tomorrow we begin trek ox, each of which costs £5. In the regiment we will get through three a day.

3 January

A shell came into the town with the following message: 'You cowards, why don't you come out and fight us in the open plain?' Rather cheek since they will not even advance to attack an outpost.

4 January

WHITE: My force here is terribly reduced in efficiency by disease and there is more enteric and dysentery every day. I have before me our sick report of one month ago. The total sick and wounded then was 436, today the total is 1,578. A month ago, 1 December, there were 29 cases of enteric fever; today there are 506 besides 285 not yet diagnosed. On 1 December we had only 76 cases of dysentery; today we have 588.

61

5 January

SHARP: On the night of 5-6 January one 4.7-in gun was moved from Junction Hill to Wagon Hill, with Gunner Sims in charge, and Engineer Sheen to mount it. A company of Gordons was sent as escort and working party.

6 January

CHICHESTER: So we were not relieved for Christmas by Sir Redvers. He seems to be sticking in the mud frightfully at Colenso. Goodness knows how long he has been there now. Am now in hospital with fever, so please excuse bad writing as I am in bed. I have been out here since 23 December and am all right now, only I am fed on milk like the rest of them and not allowed to get up yet. I hope to be back in camp in a week or ten days. I don't think I shall get back before then. The hospital is situated about 5 miles along the railway line from Ladysmith at the first station. A train is allowed to come out in the morning and go back in the evening. We have no news at all as to what happens. They are simply living on bare rations in camp now, nothing else: ½-lb of trek ox, half a loaf of bread. Out here they keep me on milk and filthy beef tea made from trek-ox. In camp you simply have to have your beef stewed for about 6 hours before you can get your teeth through it.

This is the second letter I have written you. I wish when the line is open you would send me up a nice big cake and some crystallised fruit because I haven't had a Christmas feed at all and I could eat anything now. Velcoup will bring it all up if you give it him.

THE BOER ATTACK

They are bombarding like fun today and have been at it for about 4 hours on end now. One of their 6-in guns is quite close behind the hospital, about half a mile, and makes an infernal row when she goes off. All their 6-in guns use black powder. They have only got two here left now, thank goodness. I wish Buller would hurry up. Everybody is awfully savage with him for being so long, but I suppose he knows what he is doing.

Rum show about those two batteries of artillery, wasn't it? We heard Buller has got them all back out of the river as the Boers couldn't take them away. By Jove what a feed I could do! Now I am as thin as a weasel too, with nothing but bones and skin.

FORBES: The Boers were strongly reinforced and determined to take Ladysmith at all costs. They attacked Wagon Hill and Caesar's Camp. The Transvaalers advanced on Caesar's Camp through the neutral ground at Intombi under cover of darkness and left all their boots at the bottom of the heights. Then they climbed the hill which is practically a precipice with rocks and trees. The ground on top is flat and covered with big rocks.

Our troops on Caesar's Camp were the 1st Manchesters in sangars with outposts, a small detachment of the Border Rifles, the 42nd Battery RFA, one Naval gun and two smaller ones. On Wagon Hill were half a battalion of the 1st King's Royal Rifles, a detachment of the Imperial Light Horse and a working party of two companies of the Gordons. This party was engaged in mounting 4.7-in and 12-pr Naval guns on the end of Wagon Hill.

The Boers got up to the outposts of the Manchesters and Volunteers on Caesar's Camp by saying 'Friend' when challenged, adding: 'Don't shoot we are the town guard.' Then they rushed our outposts, killed nearly the whole lot and took possession of the whole ridge round the hill.

The Gordons were called up as reinforcements to Caesar's Camp, G Company under Carnegie were ordered to assist on the left, and occupied a sangar on the left spur. The 53rd Battery RFA had by that time come into position on the low ground east of Maiden Castle. They immediately fired on the Boers who were all up to the east face of Caesar's Camp and did great execution with shrapnel, firing 450 rounds.

Long Tom on Bulwana opened fire on them and fired 90 rounds, only killing one man.

Hunt Grubbe of the Manchesters came up to Carnegie and said he would go forward to the outpost line and see if they wanted any help. He went alone unarmed and walked right up to the sangars where he was collared by the Boers. They made him sit down and they commenced firing on Carnegie who bravely led his men on, our shrapnel bursting among them. Carnegie rushed up with fixed bayonets and got within 10 yards. Colour-Sergeant Pryce who brought up a half-company killed a Boer and was immediately knocked over mortally wounded by a shell. Hit in the stomach, neck and legs, they rescued Hunt Grubbe who was then minus his belt and field glasses. Then commenced tremendous firing. Carnegie shot four Boers dead, we had two of G Company killed and many wounded. Then Carnegie was hit in the arm and neck and carried to the rear.

In the meantime the Rifle brigade had gone up and rein-forced the firing line, driving the enemy off the top. Our firing line was then all along the crest with the Boers down below and coming up the side. They had excellent cover and sat behind stones shooting at our men. We moved up to the Manchester Camp at 10.30 and almost immediately sent Macready with A Company up to the firing line where he sat all day. B Company followed him in support as did late in the evening D Company under Sellar. Firing went on the whole day long.

THE FIGHTING ON WAGON HILL

PEARSE: The Imperial Light Horse deserve every distinction that can be given them for having saved the force on Wagon Hill from a very serious calamity, if not actual disaster. They must share the credit, to some extent, however, with two small bodies of men who happened to be on Wagon Hill neither for fighting nor watch-keeping – the few blue-jackets of HMS *Powerful* in charge of the big gun which had been brought up that night for mounting there, and the handful of Royal Engineers under Lieuts. Digby-Jones and Dennis, preparing the necessary epaulements for that weapon. When firing began, the gun still being on its wagon, all that could be done was to outspan its team of oxen. Then blue-jackets and sappers, seizing each his rifle, took their places behind slight earthworks, prepared to fight it out manfully.

(In the afternoon a party of Boers was still in possession of a crest about 100 yards below the Imperial Light Horse redoubt on the west of the hill. They had been holding on all day and inflicting great loss, and it had been impossible to dislodge them. Three companies of the Devons were called up to reinforce our men on Wagon Hill).

JACSON: Lieut.-Colonel C.W. Park was asked if he could turn the Boers out by rushing them with the bayonet. He answered: 'We will try'. After the three companies had been formed up in column with bayonets fixed and magazines charged, Colonel Park gave the order to advance at fifty paces interval in quick time, and when the top of the ridge was reached to charge the position occupied by the Boers.

The charge took place in a blinding hailstorm, a time well chosen, as the hail was beating into the faces of the Boers. The men, before reaching the place where they formed up for the charge, were wet through and had put on their warm coats which they had carried strapped on to their belts.

When the storm was at its height, Colonel Park gave the order to charge. Lieut. Field, who commanded the leading company, rushed forward up the slope, shouting, 'Company, double charge!' He was immediately followed at a distance of about ten yards by Masterson's company, which was immediately followed by Lafone's. On they went to reach their goal, 130 yards away, over perfectly flat open ground.

SELBY: A moment's lull, as of surprise, then the Boers poured a volley into them. Next, springing to their feet they emptied their magazines into the advancing line. But the line, though

65

sadly thinned, never wavered, never checked. Swerving a little to the right to come directly on their enemy, prolonged on either side by the Imperial Horse and cavalrymen and 60th, who were inspired by their example, they swept the Boers finally from the hill. Everywhere they rushed down the slopes to the rear.

THE DIVERSIONARY ATTACK

(While the main battle thus raged on the southern perimeter of the Ladysmith defences, the Boers mounted a diversionary attack in the north.)

NEVINSON: The Boers began their attack on Observation Hill just before dawn with a rapid fire of guns and rifles at long range. At first only our guns replied, the two of the 69th Battery doing excellent work with shrapnel over the opposite ridges. By about 6 am we could see the Boers creeping forward over Bell Spruit and making their way up the dongas and ridges in our front. At about 8 am there was a pause, and it seemed as if the attack was abandoned, but it began again at 9 with greater violence. The shell fire was terrific. Every kind of shell from the 45-pr of the 4.7-in howitzer down to the 1½-pr of the automatic was hurled against those little walls, while shrapnel burst almost incessantly overhead.

It is significant for our own use of artillery that not a single man was killed by shells, though the air buzzed with them. The loose stone walls were cover enough. But the demoralizing effect of shell fire is well known to all who have stood it. A good regiment is needed to hold on against such a storm. But the Devons are a good regiment – perhaps the best here now – and, under the command of Major Curry, they held.

WHITE: After a very obstinate fight which lasted from 2.30 am till 7.30 in the evening, we defeated the Boers everywhere with great loss. At times I was very anxious but the troops on the whole behaved well, though one or two Corps have had too much of it and are not what they were. Ian Hamilton was

66

in command where the principal attack was made and did invaluable service. Everybody under him is full of his praise, and I have reported on him in the highest terms.

Some of the Boers showed most determined bravery. An old man, one of their leaders, stalked up a steep hillside and with a few followers, put their rifles over the parapet of one of our works and shot some of the officers and men in it dead, including Major Miller-Wallnutt of the Gordons. These Boers were I believe all killed but they drove our people back for a time. We handed over their dead to the Boers next morning (Sunday 7th), and as each succeeding hero was brought down – they *were* heroes – the Boers wrung their hands and owned that we had killed their best.

7 January

FORBES: The Boers were told to come and collect their dead. We took 49 bodies down off the left of Caesar's Camp and laid them in the scrub. Sixty-seven were collected down below, and at Bester's Farm about 40 were laid out in a row.

The chief came round at noon and said: 'The Gordons have saved the day.' A special issue of rum was allowed and congratulations on our gallantry sent round as we have gained a victory which was the turning point and most critical day of the whole campaign. In the evening we got the awful news that our dear Colonel was dead.

The Boers of the Heidelberg contingent who were attacking us had a Commandant and three Field-Cornets killed. The Commandant had a message from Joubert in his pocket which read: 'Ladysmith must be captured at all costs'.

At 5.00 pm there was a funeral just south of the Manchesters' camp; there were over 30 bodies laid out and the three denominations read out their services. We then sprinkled earth over each body and left the Kaffirs to put them into the long trench they were digging. It was awful seeing those poor fellows. They were in all sorts of attitudes as they could not be straightened out. One was in the correct kneeling position for firing.

67

The Boer Commandant de Villiers was killed. De Villiers had his nephew fighting with the Imperial Light Horse. Next day Fitzgerald went out with the Boer Commander. He was such a nice old gentleman and when he took the handkerchief off de Villiers' face he wept like a child.

The battle on Saturday was nearly lost on account of the following awful facts. There were 10 weeks and plenty of men and materials to put the whole of the hills in an absolute state of defence, but all they did was to dig some big forts back from the crest. There were no attempts made to fortify the crests, a few rotten little sangars were built but were quite useless. No field of fire was cleared and no trenches made or even cover for the men. Though there were hundreds of coils of barbed wire there, no obstacles of any sort were made. The whole place could have been made absolutely impregnable and could easily have been held by one battalion. It is monstrous and disgraceful that so many lives should have been thrown away just because these small precautions were disregarded.

11 January

The big Boer gun did not fire all day. We cannot understand it at all. There has been a great deal of movement among the Boers all round today. They have been digging hard everywhere, improving their trenches, putting up fortifications, etc. Also two guns and large reinforcements left for Colenso, numbers of wagons have been on the move. This is the day a battle is expected and Buller hopes to advance.

Besters, who had a farm under Wagon Hill, has five sons fighting against us. He owns 40,000 acres in Natal. On Saturday evening the very Irish doctor of the Manchesters went to the signal station and in a very loud voice before a crowd of soldiers dictated the following message: 'Don't be anxious darling only a flesh wound in the forearm not dangerous love and kisses to yourself Rita and mother.' The message as heliographed was reduced to the one word: 'Fit!'

WHITE: I know that Buller is advancing with a force which I estimate at near 30,000 men to attempt to cross the Tugela and relieve Ladysmith. I only wish I could help him but my force is terribly reduced, principally by loss of officers in action. I could not leave a garrison sufficiently strong to defend Ladysmith and move out to help Buller with more than 3,000 men. Even if I abandoned Ladysmith altogether I would not be able to march out with 8,000 men. The Boers would follow me up with at least this number, and as they are all mounted, they could get round me. I would also have to deal with the enemy in front of me.

I have therefore to play what to me is the painful part of sitting quietly in Ladysmith awaiting the success of Buller's force. If he is repulsed again we shall be in a bad way. I dread to think of what the effect on our Cause would be if Ladysmith is reduced by famine or taken by assault. The Boers have spent their chief force on the conquest of Natal and Ladysmith has so far held them. If they take Ladysmith with its garrison and guns it will be a blow that it will be very difficult for our Empire to recover from. I believe it would be sound to devote all our efforts to conquering Joubert here, even if we have to bring another division here, but placed as I am I cannot say this. The fall of Ladysmith would do more to aid the Dutch cause in the Cape Colony than Methuen and Gatacre being held in their present positions for another 3 – 4 weeks.

13 January

NEVINSON: Most of us have agreed never to mention the word 'Buller', but it is hard to keep that pledge.

14 January

WHITE: This Sunday, one appreciates a day of rest when it means freedom from the boom boom fizz of 6-in shells. On Friday we had the pleasure to see the helio to the south-west of us and know that it meant that Sir Redvers was approaching us via Potgieters Drift over the Tugela. He is not communicative but so far everything appears to promise well this time. This morning I hear that G.W. Steevens the correspondent and author of 'With Kitchener to Khartoum' and other works is very bad. He has been laid up with enteric and was getting much better, but he has had a relapse and has now some very bad symptoms.

We have been listening for Buller's guns but have not heard them. I thought he might have a Sunday fight, but I am now glad he has not as the Boers consider Providence is against the side that forces a battle on the Sabbath.

15 January

FORBES: Got all my photographs developed. They have all come out so well. I am very pleased with them. It is said that a composite regiment of cavalry is being made out of the brigades to cut off the Boers retreating from Buller. Great care has been taken in selecting horses that will not fall down when a man mounts and that when the man is up they will be able to travel at least three miles. It is at present very doubtful whether a regiment as a whole can be raised.

BULLER CROSSED THE TUGELA RIVER AT TRICKHARDT'S DRIFT.
BRITISH HEAVY ARTILLERY ON MOUNT ALICE,
SOUTH OF THE RIVER AND 16 MILES FROM LADYSMITH.
STARTED TO BOMBARD BOER POSITIONS

17 January

SHARP: Heavy firing to the southward; everyone hoping to be relieved within the week. Bulwana, Surprise Hill and a host of smaller guns firing all day.

FORBES: At 9.00 pm a special order came out to say that the flying column was to be ready to turn out at a moment's notice after midnight, taking one day's rations on pack mules.

70

18 January

SHARP: Bulwana fired a good bit during the forenoon; the relief column shells can be seen bursting on Roodepoort Ridge. John, A.B. was killed by a shrapnel bullet from the high velocity gun on Pepworth, while asleep in his tent.

NEVINSON: The market quotations at this evening's auction were fluctuating. Eggs sprang up from 1 guinea to 30 shillings a dozen. Jam started at 30 shillings the 6-lb jar. On the other hand tobacco fell: Egyptian cigarettes were only one shilling each and Navy Cut went for four shillings an ounce. During a siege one realises how much more than bread, meat and water is required for health. Flour and trek ox still hold out, and we receive the regulation short rations. Yet there is hardly one of us who is not tortured by some internal complaint, and many die simply for want of common little luxuries. In nearly all cases where I have been able to try the experiment I have cured a man with any little variety I had in store or could procure – rice, chocolate, cake, tinned fruit, or soups. Men and horses crawl feebly about, shaken with every form of internal pain and weakness. Women suffer even more. The terror of the shells has caused 32 premature births since the siege began.

FORBES: Buller's guns kept firing all night and all today. From Wagon Hill one could see the firing – our shells, as Maud the correspondent said, seemed to take the top off the mountains. As far as is gathered the Boer positions and laager have been severely shelled and the Boers have been trekking. From Wagon Hill it took 52 seconds for the sound to reach us after the burst was seen which makes the distance 10½ miles. Many wagons have been seen going towards Van Reenen's Pass.

The want of footwear in some regiments is very bad. The men of the Manchesters were seen grubbing in the artillery refuse pits for boots.

Eggs are now 22 shillings a dozen. Cigarettes 80 shillings a

71

hundred. The corporal of ours who is in charge of the military prison has made £50 by the sale of shells.

19 January

Sir George is seedy. We have 120 officers on the sick list here. 68 officers killed and wounded. The Boers have all been on the move and seem to be concentrating on the north side. The flying column is not on, being only a ruse to annoy the Boers.

WHITE: I had a note from General Geoffrey Barton, dated 14 January, from Chieveley, in which he said: 'Lady White's prodigious supplies for your troops are at Estcourt.' So I presume you have been turning your great energy to promoting aid for our poor fellows. If there are any goods that could be used as medical comforts I wish I had them here. I have, or had on the 17th. 741 cases of enteric and 451 suspected cases not yet diagnosed. As two thirds of the latter will probably turn out to be enteric it makes a total of over 1,000 cases. I doubt if any one hospital ever before contained such a record.

20 January

FORBES: Was nearly driven daft by the excessive heat and flies. Usual day on picquet. Several Boer waggons on the move. Watched the shelling on the ridge by the Tugela. It was quite splendid to see. The shells kept on bursting all along the ridge about five miles away at an average rate of four a minute between 1.00 pm and 6.00 pm, both shrapnel and common. They were well burst raking the ridge on this side splendidly. The Boer laager and ridge were set on fire. A message came through to say that everything was going on well and that relief was certain. On the strength of this news we had the company for dinner.

22 January

Buller has signalled that all is going well: 'I do not want your assistance. My guns are not all bark but a great deal of bite.' Firing has been seen only about three miles from the south-east of Bulwana. Ward had a heliogram from Morgan saying that he has a large column of luxuries ready to be pushed in here as soon as possible.

A poem re Ladysmith:
'Ladysmith thou art supremely cussed
with flies, bad water and with dust
a filthy fever-stricken nest
with no redeeming feature blest'.

by Robert King. 31/12/99.

Our return of sick and wounded at Intombi:
15 cases of enteric, 2 of dysentery and total 44, the remainder being wounded.

Several Russian officers have resigned their commissions in order to join the Boers.

SHARP: Heavy firing heard more to the northward. Payne, A.B. and Stroker Wheeler were killed while attempting to open a 6-inch shell in the town strictly against the Captain's orders.

23 January

All our guns opened a heavy fire on the Boer's position in order to prevent them going to reinforce the Boers opposing Buller. Bulwana opened fire just after 8.00 am.

The camp is being prepared against Bulwana.

FORBES: At about 5.00 am all our guns opened a tremendous fire all round the perimeter. This is an idea of Rawlinson's in order to see how many Boers there were round here and distract their attention from Buller. A most awful affair and cruel waste of ammunition and did no good.

Bran has been cut from the mules in order to make up the deficiency in the flour. The crying shame is that a number of wagons have been loaded up with food in order to feed Buller! A nice job for a starving garrison to do! This is KCB hunting by the authorities at our expense.

73

WHITE: Buller's guns are still heard every day in the distance. Native deserters from the enemy's lines round us say the Boers are beginning to be frightened. The big guns he has with him create a great impression. Joubert, and consequently the headquarters of the Armies of the South African Republics are still here. I was right when, months ago, I said Ladysmith would be the strategical point of the War. I now hope that before the end of January these armies will have received their first really important defeat and will commence to retrace their steps, the Free State Army towards Harrismith and the Transvaalers towards Laing's Nek. This house is now full of sick officers. I have been constantly ill myself of late—fever and inside troubles.

CHICHESTER: Am recovering from enteric and going home invalided in *Powerful* in about a fortnight when we shall probably start. Buller has not relieved us yet but is very close. In a week I shall be up, tomorrow I start on food and chuck milk. I have been in bed on milk for a month. As soon as the line is open do please send me up some rice or sponge cakes and a couple of tins of mixed sweet biscuits, as I shall be allowed them, but not the other things I asked you for except some chocolates. I don't know where you are but hope to see you before we leave. We are going down to Durban about 10 days or a fortnight after Buller comes in.

THE BATTLE OF SPION KOP

24 January

SHARP: About 3.00 am Buller started firing and kept it up till about 10.30. An infantry attack is said to be in progress. Spion Kop was captured by the relieving force. Little firing here today.

NEVINSON: From Observation Hill one could see the British shells bursting along this ridge all morning, as well as in the midst of the Boer tents halfway down the double peaks, and at the foot of the hill. The firing began at 3.00 am and lasted with extreme severity till noon, the average of audible shells being at least five a minute. We could also see the white bursts of shrapnel from our field artillery. In the afternoon I went to Wagon Hill and with the help of a telescope made out a large body of men – about 1,000 I suppose – creeping up the distant crests and spreading along the summit. I could only conjecture them to be English from their presence on the exposed ridge, and from their regular and widely extended formation. They were hardly visible except as a series of black points. Thunder-clouds hung over the Drakensberg behind, and the sun was obscured. Yet I had no doubt in my own mind that the position was won. It was 5 o'clock or a little later.

Others saw large parties of Boers fleeing for life up dongas and over plains, the phantom carriage and four driving hastily north-westwards after an urgent warning, and other such melodramatic incidents, which escaped my notice. The position of the falling shells, and the movement of those minute black specks, were to me enough drama for one day's life.

FORBES: Walked up the flagstaff and saw the shelling. Very wearisome day in camp indeed. Hot and flybegotten. Everyone in very bad temper.

25 January

News came in last night that Buller had captured the left of the position – Tabanyama.

NEVINSON: In the afternoon the situation was rather worse. We saw the shelling begin again, but no progress seemed to be made. About 4.00 pm we witnessed a miserable sight. Along the main track which crosses the great plain and passes round the end of Telegraph Hill, almost within range of our guns, came a large party of men tramping through the dust. They were in khaki uniform, marched in fours, and kept step. Undoubtedly, they were British prisoners on their way to Pretoria. In front and rear trudged an unorganised gang of Boers, evidently acting as escort. It was a miserable and depressing thing to see.

26 January

FORBES: Out of 12,000 fighting men in Ladysmith 4,000 have passed through or are in Intombi. Medicines are now practically finished so the suffering of the sick has increased. Most regiments can only turn out about 450 strong.

WHITE: The last few days have been ones of great anxiety to us. On the morning of 24th Buller's guns poured a heavy bombardment on Tabanyama and I knew that he meant to attack. His signallers are not good and we have not been kept well up in what is going on, but a message, only partly received owing to a breakdown in their lamp arrangements, is not encouraging. I suggested to Buller that if he had any doubt of success, he should ask Roberts for further reinforcements and not risk the attack until he was very sure of success. I told him Ladysmith would be in a bad way if he tried and failed, but that I could, I thought, defend myself here for another month. From his answer I conclude he did not act on my suggestion.

I believe two divisions, the 6th and 7th, have both arrived this month at Cape Town. Surely one of these could be spared for the relief of Ladysmith.

I have since volunteered to make an effort from this side to help Buller. I told him my force was greatly played out but that we would do our best if he would let me know his plans so that I might co-operate. He declined my offer and said he would let me know if I could help him. The fall of Ladysmith would be a *terrible* blow to England's prestige. It would have even a worse effect in India where they know nothing of the strength of our Navy and of the influence of sea power. The fact that I, a late Tangi Lord Sahib have had to haul down my flag to an unknown – so far as India at large is concerned – power would shake India's belief in British power. Coupled to that, it would be known that Lord Roberts Sahib,

76

who is held throughout the length and breadth of India to represent England's military power, was in command and could not save us. The whole of the troops sent from India are here with their native followers, and there are besides some hundreds of natives of India who have been employed in Natal and the Transvaal and who have taken refuge here.

27 January

SHARP: A little firing here today. Still too thick for helio-graphing till the evening when we got a message: 'Warren's troops took Spion Kop, held it all day but lost it that night'. This looks as though relief was further off than ever.

FORBES: It is true that Buller has taken the knock again. It seems that he took the centre kopje "Spion Kop" at 7.00 pm on Wednesday (24 January). The next morning the Boers and British both thought that the other had the hill. However the Boers got it. All their laagers are back again.

A Kaffir deserter came in and said that Kaffirs were holding the Boers' horses below their lines at Spion Kop and got shelled so they jumped on their backs and galloped off to the British lines with about 500 of them.

28 January

The Boers at Spion Kop strongly reinforced. A large laager outspanned by the Colenso road near white rocks and remained all day. At 4.00 pm they had a prayer meeting, about 500 of them. After this one buggie drove off with a tremendous big escort. People say it was Kruger himself who had come to preach. Several other big bugs drove off in buggies and escorted and at 6.00 pm they laagered up, inspanned and the whole lot went off towards Spion.

WHITE: If Buller's force had held Spion Kop we should have reached the turning point in the war. I know how apt one is to criticize unfairly unless one knows all particulars but the message suggests two things to me. It was easier to hold Spion Kop than to gain possession of it in the first place. It should have been strongly reinforced with unshaken troops. Secondly, 500 casualties was a very small price to pay for the capture of the key of a position which would have made the way to Ladysmith easy. Out of my small force I lost over 400 in the Boer attack on Caesar's Camp and Wagon Hill on the 6th. We must make up our minds to greater losses if we are to beat enemies like the Boers.

My position here is now critical. I believe I can defend Ladysmith so long as my provisions last; but my troops are already on short rations and so are my horses, both are therefore losing strength daily. But when my provisions are out I am done for. I have now put the situation fully before Buller and asked him to refer to Roberts. If no more reinforcements can be sent to Buller and he does not succeed in getting to Ladysmith there only remains the rather desperate alternative of abandoning Ladysmith and trying to fight my way through to join his force. I should of course dislike intensely giving up Ladysmith to the enemy after having defended it so long.

I feel that I have done all that could be done. The full force of the invaders, both Transvaalers and Free Staters first burst upon me. I have barred the way to them by every means in my power and I succeeded in holding them until Maritzburg and the Colony of Natal South of it was safe. Buller's fights with the Boers and also the fights in the Cape Colony have shown what a difficult enemy they are to conquer. I unaided had the headquarters of both Armies to deal with. At Talana Symons beat them. At Elandslaagte I defeated them thoroughly. At Rietfontein they attacked me but made no impression on me and dared not follow me when I had to return to Ladysmith. At Lombard's Kop I drove them back and on the 6th January I routed them utterly. I also defeated them in a former attack on Ladysmith. Nicholson's Nek was therefore the only occasion on which they defeated my force and the troops there were a mere detachment.

78

29 January

FORBES: Buller's searchlight on all night and three of the enemy's on here. Losses of officers during the siege: 44 killed, 11 died of wounds.

30 January

Food supplies are now very low. Only 2½ commissariat biscuits a day and meat which is a mixture of horse, mule and trek ox; ¾-oz of tea – no bread left, very poor grub, all our stores are through. The cavalry horses, our horses and mules now get no rations at all. Only the gunner horses and mules are being fed. The cavalry horses grazing all day. Not much grass and they are awfully thin.

NEVINSON: Today was certainly the gloomiest in all the siege. It rained steadily night and morning, the steaming heat was overpowering, and we sludged about, sweating like the victims of a foul turkish bath. Towards evening it suddenly turned cold. Black and dismal clouds hung over all the hills. The distance was fringed with funereal indigo. The wearied garrison crept through their duties, hungry and gaunt as ghosts. There was no heliograph to cheer us up and hardly a sound of distant guns. The rumour had got abroad that we were to be left to our fate whilst Roberts, with the main column, diverted all England's thoughts to Bloemfontein. Like one man we lost our spirits, our hopes and our tempers.

One of the chief difficulties for Colonel Ward and Colonel Stoneman is the large body of Indians – bearers, sais, bakers, servants of all kinds – who came over with the troops and will not eat the sacred cow. Out of about 2,000 only 487 will consent to do that. The remainder can only get very little rice and mealies. Their favourite ghee, or clarified butter, has entirely gone, and their hunger is pitiful. The question now is whether their religious scruples will allow them to eat horse.

31 January

FORBES: Parliament opens today. Buller's two messages will doubtless be read: they are to the best of my belief as follows: *Wednesday* evening: 'I have taken a hill from which I can relieve Ladysmith in 6 hours.' *Thursday* morning: 'The hill has been disgracefully abandoned by the regiment holding it.' Price of eggs at the market yesterday: 37 shillings and sixpence a dozen. Chickens £1 each.

We have two working parties out tonight, the idea being that Rawlinson thinks if the Boers see us making great works all round that they will thereby be drawn off Buller.

1 February

Rode out across the river by the end of Caesar's camp to the farm which is close to Intombi. Found 50 bags of 200 lbs each of flour which we commandeered.

A large number of cavalry horses shot and may died from starvation.

2 February

SHARP: Horse soup 'Chevril' is to be served out to the troops from today.

NEVINSON: 'Mind that stuff, it kicks,' says the British soldier, as he carries it away.

The Chevril was produced by Lieutenant McNalty of the ASC in an apparatus of his own invention in the railway station engine shed.

Three or four messages came through on the heliograph, but who could have guessed the thrilling importance of the first? It ran: 'Sir Stafford Northcote, Governor of Bombay, has been made a peer.'

FORBES: Sergeant Patterson was sent up to Wagon Hill to snipe at Boers. He killed four and one pony at 2,100 yards, which is pretty fair, using the dial sight.

Up to 16 January our wounded were 137 officers and 1,201 rank and file. Total killed were 40 officers and 550 rank and file.

3 February

Stood to arms before dawn and awaited the expected attack which never came off. Relief is expected within eight days.

WHITE: I have heard from Roberts in reply to my telegram to Buller. He compliments us on our heroic defence, but will not send any reinforcements to Natal. He says he hopes to relieve the pressure on Ladysmith by his operations in the Orange Free State before the end of February. I believe the Boers have from the first so set their hearts on conquering Natal that they will hold out here to the very end. They say – so our spies tell us – they have come here 'to conquer or to die.' I will therefore do all in my power to keep the English flag flying here as long as I can and will not abate one precaution in reliance on being helped either by Roberts or by Buller. I have therefore reduced the rations in some items down to starvation level. The officers and men only get ½ lb of bread daily. When there are no vegetables or anything else to supplement it, ½ lb of bread is very little. To make up for the deficiency I give the men horse flesh. The beef is very hard, trek-ox; the horse flesh is not bad but I am too fastidious to eat it. Many of the officers prefer it to the hard bad beef. The soldier gets 1/6 oz tea, 1 oz sugar, ½-oz salt, 1/64 oz pepper, 1/20 oz mustard and 1/10 gill vinegar. The men are listless and in some cases insubordinate, refusing to work because they are not fed. We have no liquor except some light claret at the HQ mess. You may imagine the price of liquor when I say that, some time ago, a dozen of whisky sold in Ladysmith for £147, or £12.5s.0d. a bottle. I have reduced the number of cavalry horses that receive a grain ration to 300. The rest of the horses have to graze and will be useless for cavalry.

4 February

FORBES: It seems absolutely certain that there is to be an attack here tonight. Very great precautions have been taken. Great systems of sangars have been made all along the ridge.

81

The guns on Caesar's Camp have been loaded up with case and depressed on to the plain. Tar barrels have been placed out on the plain ready to be lighted to show up the Boers. Rockets are to be sent up in case of attack to inform Buller so that he can also attack if we are in difficulties. Patrolling system rearranged and perfected. Countersign changed at midnight. The Boers are expected to come up to our patrols dressed in British uniforms with braces, belts and pouches and speaking English.

The staff seem to have received absolute information that the relief will certainly come this week. Medicines are now at an end and men are dying mainly for want of them.

5 February

As I was sitting in my bath the cry of Long Tom came unpleasantly when I was covered with soap. I could not get out and run so sat still and bang went the gun and swish bang came the 100 lb shell and burst just 9 ft from where I was with a fearful explosion. The pieces went flying everywhere and one hit and went straight through the doctor's tent. My tent was covered in a cloud of earth. I got an awful fright but was absolutely unhurt.

Horse steaks and sausages are not bad at all. The stuff that people smoke now is curious: tea leaves after being used; bark; grass dried and other horrible concoctions. Our rations are awfully small; two biscuits and 1 lb of horse is about all.

BULLER'S ATTACK ON VAAL KRANTZ

5 February

Buller commenced the most awful bombardment I have ever heard, starting at dawn and going on all day. The earth was shaken and Macready got a headache from it. No news has come in at all with reference to it.

SHARP: Buller started early this morning in the direction of Potgieters Drift and fighting went on all day. A little firing here but nothing to speak of.

6 February

FORBES: The bombardment to the south and south-west went on with tremendous and awful severity. In four minutes as many as 129 heavy artillery shots were counted. This went on at this rate for many hours. One 6-in Boer gun was spotted and all of a sudden an enormous explosion took place – it must have been the magazine. Great schemes and precautions have been made re the flying column which some expect to go out.

A special issue of sausages to all troops made out of the remains of the slaughtered horses. It is said that these are good, but one is sufficient as they are so rich.

On the present scale of rations we can hold out until 7 March and then seven days more on the gun horses alone. The only news from Buller is 'RT' which means that all is going well.

Having one's bedding out on picquet so often it becomes a great receptacle for such beasts as ants, bugs, fleas etc. I had 48 bites last night but never caught one beast. The kirk yard here is full up which means about 700 poor soldiers have been laid to rest since the siege began.

SHARP: Heavy firing from Buller, but more to the eastward, began about 8 am and lasted till 11.30 am. The day was dull but fine. Lieut. Tyndale-Biscoe has got enteric and went out to Intombi. A little firing during the day.

7 February

Heavy firing from Buller's column, but more to the northward. Shells can be seen bursting beyond Middle Hill. Very little firing here today except for a few small guns.

8 February

Relief Column still firing in about the same place as yesterday very heavily. Junction Hill 4.7-in gun and the howitzers are to be moved again to Wagon Hill. It is rumoured that Mafeking has been relieved.

FORBES: This is the 100th day of complete investment. Our stores are practically through and we feed on horse and biscuit.

A civilian named Fosse has been court-martialled for creating despondency in the town. He was convicted and sentenced to one year's hard.

The Boers are driving all their cattle north. They have commandeered every man and every boy above 13 years of age to fight.

9 February

Four months ago we landed in this country. In the afternoon got orders to send 10 mules for slaughter for food. Poor beasts, I am sorry for them for they are the best in Ladysmith and are in very fair condition. Rumours: 'Buller is getting on well; Buller is getting on badly; Buller cannot advance so is waiting for Roberts to take Bloemfontein.'

SHARP: The 4.7-in is not going to be moved, but the howitzers were put in position and gave Middle Hill a few rounds. Bulwana and some small guns fired a few rounds today. No news; rations still further reduced.

10 February

Midshipman Hamilton and I came back from Intombi. I found the camp quite changed. No flies, all fortified and much cleaner.

FORBES: Awful hot today. Temperature over 100°F in the shade again. Our rations have been cut down to ½-lb of bread instead of 1-lb. This is awful and after breakfast I feel quite famished. We still have a little bacon so that with dry bread and tea is all we had. The flies are worse and worse and make a decided impression on our tempers.

The whole of the able-bodied departmental men have been formed into a corps of irregular horse.

11 February

Dixon went out with a flag of truce. The Lydenburg

Commando are still here. They are frightfully sick of the whole show. They say they lost so awfully down south that they would now give in only they are kept at it by the foreign element.

Prices are rising. Eggs 48 shillings a dozen; a 4d stick of tobacco fetched 24 shillings. 150 cigars fetched £16. The heat is awful and drives one almost mad. Food is so scarce that I feel starved all day.

The agent for Reuters started off with his Kaffir to get through. After he left we heard two shots.

12 February

The heat is again awful – 100°F in the shade. Bread ration only two slices; I am awfully hungry. I rode up to the signal station and took messages. There are 300 waiting to be sent, but the Sergeant belongs to us and we are going to get ours through first. The Boers are making an enormous dam across the Klip below Intombi. The idea is to flood the town and force us to flee to the hills and be shelled.

A fellow of the Imperial Light Horse is very ill and will have to undergo an operation. He wanted to see his wife as he is likely to die. She is down south so a flag of truce was sent out asking to be allowed to let her come in. This the Boers kindly did and she arrived tonight.

A Kaffir runner came in this morning. He got as far as Intombi with 300 private letters when he was shot through the leg, knocked down and broke his collar-bone and lost all the letters.

13 February

SHARP: Official news given out today about Buller's successes at Krantz Kloof, and notice was given that the relief will probably take place in a few days. Lord Roberts is said to have advanced into the Free State.

14 February

FORBES: Eggs up to 52 shillings a dozen now. We have bought up all the starch possible and make it into pudding by

85

cooking it with water. This is most awfully good and it does one a lot of good.

15 February

The sights here are very distressing. Men look very broken down and some unfit almost to walk with torn and dirty clothes and no boots. The horses lie down and die all over the place and are merely bags of bones. A horse and mule of my transport lay down and died today.

BULLER'S FOURTH AND FINAL ATTACK

SHARP: Heard heavy firing in Colenso direction about 2 am which lasted for half an hour. About 8 am it started again and went on till 10.30.

16 February

Heard occasional heavy guns firing outside. News that Kimberley has been relieved by General French with cavalry and artillery; also that he captured several laagers and a lot of provisions and ammunition. Little or no firing here today.

17 February

Heard occasional heavy guns in Colenso direction. News about Kimberley confirmed. Roberts at Jacobsdaal. Cronje in full retreat pursued by General Kenny. Very little firing here.

FORBES: The Boers signalled to us: 'Buller will never get through to relieve you, you had better come and have a cup of coffee with us.'

18 February

Buller commenced a fearful battle down south. People from Caesar's Camp said they saw men working on the hills which we have (supposedly) captured. However a helio came in to say that everything has gone well. This is the fourth attempt Buller has made to relieve us.

SHARP: Heard heavy firing in a south-easterly direction which lasted all day. We saw shell bursting on a high ridge beyond Intombi. Eighty hands mustered by open list and looked very fit considering. No firing here all day.

19 February

Bulwana and all guns fired a few rounds. Heard that our troops had been successful and had taken several positions yesterday. Heliograph was working on the ridge over Intombi and a large gun, apparently cordite, was firing towards evening.

FORBES: Went up to the far end of Caesar's Camp and watched the battle that was going on. Everything seems to be going on awfully well. Buller has got three positions only 6 miles from Caesar's Camp. 171 Boer waggons were seen to be trekking north also many Boers. We could see Buller's guns firing and his shrapnel bursting near the ridge in front of Caesar's Camp. Great firing, musketry and Pom-pom. They are going to move our 4.7-in and 12 pr guns up to Caesar's Camp. Saw Boer ambulance waggons galloping about.

20 February

Raining and cold at night. Several fellows have been seedy owing to the drop of some 40°F in the temperature. This is the first day the number of sick have been under 2,000. I detailed four more mules for slaughter.

SHARP: Very quiet day, no news from outside. The bread gets worse every day; absolutely uneatable today.

21 February

Several heliograph messages in today but not yet published. Heavy firing outside. Bulwana and small guns fired a good deal today. Midshipman Carnegie's 12-pr was moved to the eastern end of Caesar's Camp.

FORBES: A big fight going on down at Colenso, it is believed with complete success. Lyddite shells have been seen bursting on Colenso flats not 8,000 yards from Caesar's Camp. Our Naval 12-pr which was fixed up on Caesar's Camp opened up on the bridge below Intombi and scattered the men. Bulwana fired 13 shots at our gun doing no harm.

22 February

WHITE: Buller has not yet arrived, but I believe he will be here before long. He sent me a message yesterday that he expected to be in Ladysmith today. I warned him that the enemy were stronger between him and me than he supposed. Today he flashed that he was too sanguine but that he is progressing. I expect him about Sunday; this is Thursday. On the strength of my belief in his approach I have allowed the men ½-lb more bread in hopes that I may not have to hold Ladysmith so long.

With reference to your kind gifts to the Ladysmith garrison a Natal paper proposes that Ladysmith should be rechristened Ladywhite.

There is an extraordinary case of a Sergeant Bosswell, Royal Field Artillery. On 6 January a shell struck him as he was sitting on the trail of his gun and took one leg and one arm off. He had to have the stumps of both amputated. When he was struck down he called to the men working the gun, in whose way he fell 'Here, roll me out of the way and go on with the work!' He must have a most extraordinary constitution for in about a fortnight he was out driving and does not even look pale.

SHARP: Very good news. Buller has taken several important positions and is getting on well. Lord Roberts has Cronje surrounded about 30 miles from Jacobsdaal. Bulwana fired on our 12-pr on Caesar's Camp and gave them a very hot time blowing away one side of the gun pit. The 12-pr fired several shots at a party of Boers working on a dam in the river just below Intombi.

FORBES: The daily bread ration has been increased to 1-lb which is quite splendid as I have been most fearfully hungry all day. A good thing for pudding is violet powder which makes excellent blancmange.

23 February

Buller seems to have been fighting all day. No news has come in as to what he has done.

Feel much better on full ration of biscuit.

24 February

As the men are somewhat sick, horse mince will no longer be drawn as it is unwholesome.

SHARP: Heard very heavy firing outside and could see the shells bursting on a ridge to the left of Table Hill.

25 February

FORBES: Saw the Boers building a dam across the Klip. An engine and trucks came up and brought mud. Our guns fired at it immediately and made one good shot. Everything very quiet down south, but things seem to be going on very well indeed. At 6.30 marched off with 25 men to act as covering party to the wood-cutters. The men are now falling off in health a great deal. 'Only fair' is the report on our health now. The men could hardly crawl along and several fell out, though the distance was not three miles. Out at Intombi an officer offered to exchange a box of sardines for a permanent pass to the Calcutta zoo. Eggs are hardly obtainable but 5 shillings a piece is readily given. A piece of cake tobacco value 2d was sold by auction and realised 19 shillings and sixpence. Heavy musketry down south at Pieters Station. All troops on Wagon Hill under arms.

26 February

SHARP: Midshipman Chichester returned from Intombi. The Boer guns on Bulwana, Surprise Hill and Pepworth, and nearly all the smaller guns, opened fire and kept up most of the forenoon. Received unofficial news that Cronje and 8,000 men surrendered to Lord Roberts and had also lost 1,700 killed and wounded. The 8,000 turned out to be 4,000, but still excellent news. Heard very heavy firing outside, also message: 'All going well.'

27 February

Bulwana fired a good deal, mostly into the town. Two consecutive shells burst in Dunton's stores and wrecked the whole place. Surprise Hill fired a good deal but did no harm. Again today, we saw shells bursting on the ridge on the left of Table Hill. Today is Majuba Day so an attack is expected.

FORBES: Four shots from Bulwana went on to Observation Hill, a distance of 11,000 yards or 6¼ miles – pretty good shooting. Saw the shells bursting down south – a Long Tom firing on Grobelaar Mountain. Shells bursting at Nelthorpe Station. All seems to be going well.

The rations reduced again which is awful. Only 1¼ biscuits and 3 oz of mealies. The Viceroy of India signalled in to White that the troops are wanted back on account of the unrest on the Afghan frontier.

28 February

Usual work. Did not go out as I was not very fit and also very hungry. At about midday Long Tom fired one shot. The man on the bridge did not spot where he was pointing and the shell came bang over the mess tent and went into the river. This was absolutely his last shot and we are highly honoured by the attention. At 2.00 pm we saw a derrick being put up and our guns opened fire on it making some excellent shooting.

SHARP: At 1.00 pm we received the following excellent news. 'I beat the Boers thoroughly yesterday and believe they are in full retreat. I am sending out my cavalry as quick as the bad state of the roads will permit to ascertain their whereabouts.' We saw horsemen, spring carts, wagons, three artillery guns and a good many head of cattle all galloping as hard as they could to the northward. A string of these continued all the evening. We saw the Boers trying to shift Bulwana Ben, the 6-in gun. We opened fire from our Cove

1. Cadet Edward George Chichester,
1897

2. Midshipman Charles Reynolds
Sharp, 1900

3. Lieut.-General Sir George White,
VC, Colonel, the Gordon
Highlanders

4. Lieut. Ian Foster Forbes, Gordon
Highlanders

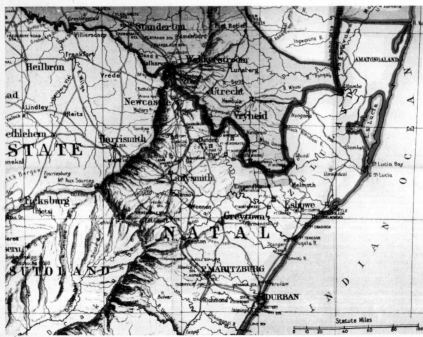

5. Ladysmith on 30th October, 1899, after the battle of Lombard's Kop. Photograph by Horace Nicholls, from the Royal Photographic Society Collection

6. Natal in 1899, from a map by George Philip & Son, Ltd. The exposed nature of the northern part of the colony, which made its defence against Boer attack so difficult, is well shown here

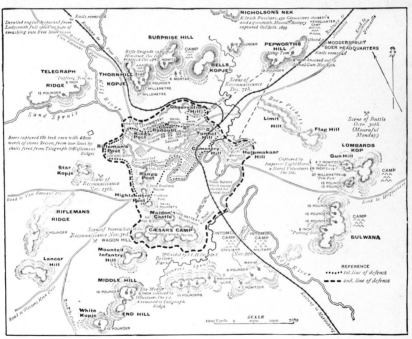

7. HMS *"Terrible"*, twin-screw cruiser, 14,200 tons, length 538 ft., beam 71 ft. 6 in. draught 27 ft., speed 22½ knots. *"Terrible"* and her sister-ship *"Powerful"* were both launched in 1895. Edward Chichester and Reynolds Sharp were on passage to the China Station in *"Terrible"* when war broke out in South Africa. *"Powerful"* was returning home from the Far East at the same time and the two ships met at Simonstown

8. The defences of Ladysmith. The defence perimeter measured 14 miles and only the guns brought in by the Naval Brigade had a range comparable to that of the Boer artillery

9. Capt. the Hon. Hedworth Lambton, who commanded the Ladysmith Naval Brigade '

10. Capt. Percy Scott, commanding HMS *"Terrible"*. Scott's improvisation of land mounts for naval guns at Simonstown and Durban provided long-range artillery not only for the defence of Ladysmith but also for the relief column, and other forces operating elsewhere

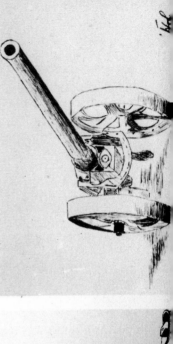

11. Naval long 12-pdr. gun on improvised land mount using Cape Waggon wheels. This actual gun was used both in the relief of Ladysmith and of the foreign legations in Peking which were besieged in the summer of 1900 by the Boxers

12,13. Drawing by Reynolds Sharp of a naval 4.7 in. gun on mobile land mount, as produced in Durban. The 4.7 in. guns taken into Ladysmith had platform mounts constructed from heavy baulks of timber, similar to that shown in plate 21

14. Indian coolie on look-out duty in Ladysmith. When the Boers opened fire he waved his flag and shouted "Long Tom"! *Photograph by Ian Forbes*

15. Mobile searchlight with "Venetian blind" shutter designed for morse signalling at Ladysmith—another adaptation by Scott of shipboard equpiment for land use. The device, forerunner of the Aldis lamp, was aimed at the clouds at night so as to "bounce" signals into Ladysmith

16. Mounting guard under fire on the Ladysmith defence perimeter.
Photograph by Ian Forbes

17. Over the difficult terrain in South Africa, before the motor transport era.
oxpower often had to be supplemented by manpower

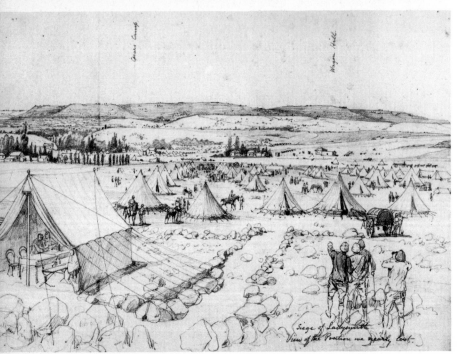

18. The camp of the 5th Lancers in Ladysmith, seen from "Cove Redoubt". The location can be found in the plan of the defences on plate 8

19. View towards the hill known as "Caesar's Camp"—"Platrand" to the Boers— scene of the Boer attack of 6th January, 1900. *Sketch by Melton Prior*

20. Heavy transport—Boer War style. A team of 16 oxen pulled 10,000 lbs, of freight. *Photograph by Ian Forbes*

21. Naval 4.7 in. gun and team with General Buller's force, at the battle of Pieters Hill, February, 1900

22. (*Opposite*) Meeting of Generals White and Buller at the Relief of Ladysmith. The spectators included Boer prisoners watching from behind bars. *From a sketch by Melton Prior in the "Illustrated London News"*

23. Sir George White's farewell to the Ladysmith garrison on 9th March, 1900. In his diary, Ian Forbes, who took this photograph, wrote: "We cheered him like anything and there was a great crowd"

24. The Ladysmith Naval Brigade marching into Windsor Castle on 2nd May, 1900 to parade before Queen Victoria

25. Reynolds Sharp on board submarine Holland 2, 1904. The five American-designed Holland boats were Britain's first submarines

26. The last Ladysmiths Officers' annual dinner was held at Claridges Hotel on 28th February, 1951 with Admiral Sir Michael Hodges in the chair. Reynolds Sharp (seated on the floor, bottom right) then aged 67, was the youngest of the party

Standing: Left to Right: Lieut.-Col. H. H. Balfour, Lieut.- Col. L. T. Goff, Major S. O. Everitt, Capt. H. A. Glen, Brig.-Gen. R. H. Kearsley, Brigadier O. S. Cameron, Col. I. R. I. F. Forbes, Col. H. A. Cape.

Centre Row: Seated: Col. W. E. Davies, Lieut.-Col. A. W. Parsons, Brig.-Gen. B. C. Dent, Col. W. Q. Winwood, Admiral A. Walker-Heneage-Vivian, Admiral Sir M. Hodges (Chairman) Lieul-Col. R. N. Hardcastle, Col. F. F. Deakin.

Seated: on floor: Brig.-Gen. A. R. Harman, Commander C. R. Sharp—the youngest: 67 years of age.

Redoubt with the 4.7; the Junction Hill 4.7 under Gunner Sims which was moved to the end of Caesar's Camp last night, and Midshipman Carnegie's 12-pr. We knocked the sheer legs down but do not seem to have got the gun. At 6.00 pm the cavalry was seen coming in over by Intombi. Cheers went up from the different camps. Two squadrons came in under Lord Dundonald of the South African Light Horse. It poured with rain all night. It was reported that about 300 Boers had off-saddled the other side of Telegraph Hill and an attack was expected, but the rain must have stopped all idea of that. It appeared afterwards that the Boers bolted without taking anything with them leaving rifles, tents, etc. behind them. The wet must have added tremendously to the discomfort of their flight.

FORBES: Ladysmith was thereby relieved after 119 days or exactly 17 weeks' siege. It was an awfully curious sensation being relieved, it made a thrill go through one. Such cheering and singing of the National Anthem. It is pitch dark, awful thunder and very heavy rain. It is all·so splendid, about 500 irregular horse are in and they look very fit and well. I can hardly realise what has occurred, four months without a single letter, it is wonderful.

1 March

At 7.00 am we got orders to parade for a flying column to chase the Boers who are in full retreat to Elandslaagte. Three of the cavalry horses died before they got there. We then went and attacked Pepworth which was only held by a few men. We only fired 27 rounds. At 3.30 the whole show was over, the troops retired for lunch and rest. The road from the south is strewn with dead horses, broken waggons, ammunition, food and stores of all kinds. It has been a very hurried retreat.

The Bulwana gun has gone. Up there the sangar is a poor one. There are several shells left, also one of our 4.7 shells unexploded. We got a pom-pom gun at the bottom of Bulwana. Buller rode in and some of his staff. No stores in except

91

what Wright brought in for us. Felt very tired and seedy.

SHARP: 11.45 am heard that Buller was coming in. General White met him and all rode up to Headquarters together. The 13th Hussars came in with them. A long string of wagons also came in. We got full rations of biscuits, and more tea and sugar and some onions and potatoes which were a great godsend.

2 March

FORBES: A day of rest. Felt very seedy and fell down after my bath. Lay down most of the day. The supply column began to come in and in the evening we had our first supplies: an issue of jam and rum to the troops which was a very great treat. Had tea at the supply depot and got some bread and jam. Dressed for mess, I was walking over when I suddenly became so weak and dizzy that I fell down. Went to bed and had a little fever. Got a telegram from home to say they are well which is excellent. Our losses in the relief force amount to 6,000 men.

3 March

SHARP: The relief column marched in this morning; the Ladysmith garrison lined the streets. Lots of officers from the other camps came up to see us, also officers of the Naval brigade attached to the relieving force. They lost no men but had a very bad time fighting for 15 days.

We got some smokables from them, also our rations show a better figure, but no private stores to be had yet.

FORBES: Am much better, temperature normal though not very fit. The troops paraded to line the streets for the force coming in. Buller came in first looking awfully low and aged and broken down. The troops looked a splendid body of men, most with beards and looking very fine. Our pipers played each regiment past.

4 March

SHARP: Thanksgiving service this morning in the valley close to our camp. It was very impressive. The relieving force are all camped in and around the tin camp.

FORBES: I did not go to the thanksgiving service as I had a great deal of transport work. At 4 o'clock rode out to Intombi where I saw all the sick fellows I knew, then rode on to see the dam. An enormous structure made solely and entirely of sandbags – 50 yards wide and about 40 ft high. Felt rather tired so went to bed at 9.00.

5 March

A very great day indeed because the mails came in. I got 127 letters, such a splendid lot of them, so many kind friends have been writing to me. I got more letters than anyone else also a crowd of newspapers and some parcels. At 4.30 I rode up to Bulwana where Long Tom used to be. Went through the Boer camps which are all deserted now. They have been living well, beds, mattresses, tins which contained every food luxury. The view from here is curious: one cannot see our camp or any of the familiar shell traps without glasses and then only very remotely. What perfectly wonderful and marvellous shooting they made.

SHARP: Much the same as yesterday, more food coming in. The officers' canteen opened and we got a few things up.

6 March

The gun crews came back to camp today. Midshipman Carnegie arrived with them. We are leaving the two 4.7's and three 12-prs for the garrison artillery. Everyone is getting ready to leave tomorrow.

FORBES: We were cinematographed at 12 for the Palace Theatre, then after marching by the machine twice we, the officers, were photoed separately for magic lantern slides. Rode to the pay office and drew £339 odd to pay my transport Zulus. Then after lunch paid out, finished my letters and wrote to mother. Had some port after a very good dinner. Sheila sent me a very acceptable tammy and still more so some tobacco.

7 March

Immediately after breakfast we, the whole regiment, went to the station to see the Naval brigade off to England. Our band and pipers played them down and off. A division under Hunter has gone to Elandslaagte. We got ½-lb of tobacco, a pipe and a Christmas card from Lady White and some stores from the *Daily Telegraph*.

SHARP: The guns and gear went down to the station about 6 o'clock. The brigade fell in at 8.15 and marched down to the station, led by the Gordons' band. General Buller and staff, Generals Hunter and Brocklehurst and a lot more friends came to say goodbye. We started about 9.30 and stopped at Intombi to pick up officers and men. The road was very rough and hilly and we did not go more than 1½ miles an hour. The whole road was strewn with bits of shells and dead horses; the latter made the march considerably worse. We arrived at Colenso about 6.30, the train not leaving till 8.30. Six sick officers of which I was one went by train, leaving Colenso at 8, and so escaped the march through Durban. We were not sorry to get on board the transport that was to take us to Simon's Bay. The rest of the brigade arrived at 2.30 pm having breakfasted at Maritzburg. Captain Percy Scott gave luncheon to the officers, while the men also had a large spread, he having met them at the station with the men of the *Terrible* and their band. They marched through the town to the transport SS *Columbian*. We sailed about 6.00 pm.

8 March

FORBES: After work Findlay and I started off to ride to Elandslaagte. At Modder Station had a look round and saw what a hasty departure the Boers had made. There was a lot of stuff in the way of bread, mealies etc, also thousands of sandbags for the dam. Got to Elandslaagte about 1 o'clock and rode the way the regiment went that day. Saw everything just the same only covered with long grass and everything very clean. Everything had been picked up even to the empty cartridge cases. Such a change from the last time I saw it. The rocks and stones though are all blue with lead still everywhere. There is a grave covered with stones down at the bottom where our three poor fellows were buried. A long trench without any mark is, I think, where all the men are. Went over the whole place and took several photographs. The only things we found were one or two bullets, a man's pouch and some canteen covers. The horses that were shot that day are still lying there and the place smells still. Started back at 3.30 and got in at 6.30, our ponies and ourselves pretty well done for, we had ridden 30 miles. We hear that Roberts has beaten the enemy again. The Boers have gone right back to the Biggarsberg.

9 March

Very hot morning. After breakfast went to the station, the whole regiment and a guard of honour of 100 men to see Sir George off. He arrived looking very ill indeed and broke down in making a speech to the regiment. We cheered him like anything and there was a great crowd.

NOTES

Date	Source	
31 Oct	Sharp	Long Tom's position was 6,800 yards distant. This was within the range of the Naval long 12-pr and 4.7-in guns, but beyond that of the Royal Artillery's guns.

2 Nov	Sharp	In all, the Boers brought into action against Ladysmith four 155-mm Creusot guns, four 120-mm Krupp howitzers and six 75-mm Creusot field guns, besides a dozen older ones. The ranges of the larger Boer guns were 10,000, 6,000 and 5,000 yards respectively.
21 Nov	Sharp	Colonel W.G. Knox (later Major-General Sir W. Knox, Colonel-Commandant, RA, died 1916) was in charge of defences of the eastern half of the horseshoe round the town. His sector was the most vulnerable: low-lying, exposed to reverse and enfilade fire by heavy guns. It looked indefensible, yet it was never seriously attacked, thanks to the powerful defences which were constructed.
8 Dec	Forbes	The Imperial Light Horse had been raised the previous September. It was composed of Uitlanders and had been originally commanded by Colonel Scott-Chisholm, late of the 5th Lancers, who was one of 10 officers of his force killed at Elandslaagte on 21 October. The two most senior officers of the ILH in Ladysmith during the Siege were Lieut.-Colonel A. Wools-Sampson and Major W. Karri Davies, who had both been imprisoned in Pretoria after the Jameson Raid and freed

on the occasion of Queen Victoria's Diamond Jubilee in 1897. The historian of the Gordon Highlanders describes the ILH as the first and perhaps the most distinguished of the many irregular corps which fought in the war. Sir George White quoted them as perhaps the bravest men he had ever commanded.

9 Dec	Sharp	The Commander who died at Graspan was A.P. Ethelston of *Powerful*. A Naval brigade under his command was fighting with Lord Methuen's force south of Kimberley. The battle took place on 25 November and the casualties included 16 Naval officers and ratings killed. Ethelston had commanded the first Naval brigade to be landed in South Africa: on 20 October at Simonstown.
9 Dec	White	The 1st Gloucesters, 1st Royal Irish Fusiliers and 10th Mountain Battery made up Colonel Carleton's column in the Nicholson's Nek disaster, in which 37 officers and 917 men were taken prisoner.
21 Dec	Forbes	The Gordons' low sickness figures were doubtless due to the fact that they had been inoculated against enteric, an early example of mass inoculation.
27 Dec	Forbes	The "Elandslaagte guns" were

97

those captured from the Boers on 21st October.

30 Dec	Sharp	The Naval brigade with Buller's force at this stage of the relief campaign was a composite force including Natal Naval Volunteers and officers and men landed from *Forte, Philomel, Tartar* and *Terrible*. Twenty-five officers from *Terrible* served in this brigade, headed by Commander A.H. Limpus.
6 Jan	Sharp	Sharp was in hospital with dysentery at this time. His copy of the brigade's log records that the Naval casualties included Stoker Leather killed and Engineer Sheen and Able Seaman Ward wounded.
23 Jan	White	The Orange Free State and Transvaal forces' headquarters were located 3½ miles NW and 5 miles NE of the town respectively, both distances measured from the defence perimeter.
24 Jan	Nevinson	Nevinson's observation point was 15 miles from Spion Kop.
11 Feb	Forbes	Reuter's man got through safely.
12 Feb	Forbes	The man of the ILH died before his wife arrived. She was allowed to leave the town again under a flag of truce.
18 Feb	Sharp	Open list: Counting numbers actually present rather than theoretical complement.

28 Feb	Sharp	Sheer legs: Naval term for the tripod used for handling heavy parts of a gun during erection and dismantling.
		The first troops actually to enter Ladysmith were squadrons of the Imperial Light Horse and Natal Carbineers led by Capt. Hubert Gough. Gough had gone forward in spite of orders to the contrary from Lord Dundonald. Dundonald himself hurried into Ladysmith later the same evening when the news of Gough's exploit reached him. Most accounts of the relief of the town give credit to Dundonald for being the first in; in fact Gough was.
6 Mar	Forbes	The Boer War was the first war in which cine cameras were used. W.K.L. Dickson of the American Biograph Company took shots in several battle areas. The filmed episodes were brief, and were screened in the intervals of live performances at music-halls. As Forbes indicates, the movie men of those days already shot more than one 'take' if they could!
7 Mar	Sharp	The brigade had to travel by road between Intombi, where Naval personnel fit to travel were picked up, and Colenso, as the line and the bridge over the Tugela had been damaged in the fighting. This explains the reference to a

rough road in what was apparently a rail journey throughout.

CHAPTER SIX

After the Siege

LIKE so many others who went through the siege, Reynolds Sharp, Edward Chichester, Ian Forbes and Sir George White had suffered in health, and the war was finished for them. Reynolds Sharp and Sir George White were now on their way home to recuperate, and incidentally to take part in public rejoicings. Ian Forbes and Edward Chichester were invalided home a few weeks later.

It was not long before the three young officers reported for duty again – peacetime duty, until August, 1914. Their subsequent careers, and those of some of the senior officers who distinguished themselves in the Boer War or subsequently, are outlined in the next chapter.

For Sir George White the siege was the culmination of a distinguished career. When the Hero of Ladysmith arrived home he was fêted in Portsmouth and London and received by Queen Victoria, who noted in her journal:

'He looks wonderfully well, though very thin, and is so pleasant and interesting to talk to, so wonderfully modest.'

Before taking up his appointment at Gibraltar which had been delayed by the war, he toured his native Ulster where he also had an enthusiastic reception.

While in Gibraltar he was promoted to Field-Marshal. His tour of duty there came to an end in 1904, when he was appointed Governor of the Royal Hospital, Chelsea, a post which he held till his death in 1912.

An equestrian statue was erected in his honour in Portland Place, London. Every year on the anniversary of the relief, until 1970, a wreath was laid there by Boer War

Veterans, the youngest of whom was then aged 90.

★

With Ladysmith free and the Boers entrenched behind the Biggarsberg mountain range between Elandslaagte and Dundee, the Natal Field Force was reorganised and the garrison formed its IVth Division. The Gordons were placed in the 7th Brigade with the 1st Devons, 2nd Rifle Brigade and 1st Manchesters. The Brigade moved a few miles out of town to Arcadia Camp to recuperate, and returned in mid-April, refreshed.

Captain Jones's naval brigade, which had helped to relieve the town, left for Durban on 11 March. The landing party from *Terrible* rejoined their ship, Captain Percy Scott handed over to his successor as Commandant of Durban, and the cruiser sailed for the Far East on 27 March. Later the same year some of the same naval guns which had been landed for use against the Boers, went into action against the Boxers who were besieging the foreign legations in Peking.

The reorganised Natal Field Force included a Naval brigade landed from other ships and consisting of ten officers and 90 men with six naval guns.

Apart from exchanges of artillery fire on two occasions in April, all was quiet on this front until 9 May, when the Force resumed its advance towards the Transvaal. Meanwhile other forces under Lord Roberts, General French and Colonel Hamilton were also advancing on the Transvaal from Bloemfontein and Kroonstad. Mafeking was relieved on 17 May, after 217 days. On 24 May the Orange Free State was formally annexed to the British Empire; on 5 June Lord Roberts hoisted the Union Flag in Pretoria.

With the capitals of both Republics in British hands it seemed that the war must be over; but the Boers resisted doggedly for a further two years.

★

Many books about the war appeared in 1900. Some of the despatches from the journalists in Ladysmith which have been quoted in an earlier chapter, had been delayed or lost in transit. Fuller versions were now published in book form. Most of Europe backed the Boers, but there was support for Britain in the United States, and a notable American anglophile was the naval historian Captain A.T. Mahan, best known for his work 'The Influence of Sea Power on History', published in 1890. In 1900 his book 'The Story of the War in South Africa', came out.

By a remarkable coincidence, Reynolds Sharp picked up a second-hand copy in the Charing Cross Road in London which proved to have belonged to Sir George White. The owner had written a number of marginal comments in it, and these go far to explain his decision to make a stand at Ladysmith.

Mahan mentions the meeting between White and the Governor of Natal at Pietermaritzburg on 9 October 1899, at which the latter referred to 'grave political consequences' such as a rising of the natives and Boer sympathisers, which might result if British forces left Northern Natal undefended, and concentrated from the outset on the defence of Ladysmith.

'I had been through the Indian Mutiny,' writes Sir George White, 'and knew what a native rising means. Had I ignored the advice of the Governor and ordered the Dundee detachment to fall back on Ladysmith, and had that retirement been followed by a native rising and Dutch rebellion in Southern Natal, the effect would have been disastrous in a Military as in a political sense.'

All too soon, White was obliged to withdraw to Ladysmith. Mahan describes the British force shut up there as 'very strong, and while incapable of taking the field against the vastly superior numbers confronting it, most capable of embarrassing any onward movement of the enemy. This aspect of the case has been too much neglected.'

Sir George White's marginal note reads:

103

'Quite sound. The view I expressed before I was besieged. On 25 October I wired to the Governor "I most urgently request that pressure may not be put on me to reduce my force here. If I am strong here and can strike out the country is unconquered. If I am shut in here the colony is at the mercy of the enemy and will have to be reconquered from the sea".'

On the choice of Ladysmith as a place in which to make a stand, Mahan writes that it was widely regarded at the time as an unfortunate accident forced upon the British as a result of the faulty dispositions of the campaign.

Sir George White comments:

'I intended from the day I landed in Natal to fight in the open and if possible beat the enemy in the open. If I failed I would fall back behind entrenchments at Ladysmith and continue sorties as long as I could.'

Mahan, while stressing the strategic importance of Ladysmith, writes that it did not follow that the best course was necessarily to occupy the town itself or the particular lines ultimately established around it by Sir George White.

Sir George White comments: 'The best positions were undoubtedly selected, but I had to play a game of bluff and occupy an area out of proportion to my numbers to deny the positions to the enemy.'

Mahan quotes White's statements on the importance of Natal, and Ladysmith, to the Boers, which appeared in the Press after his return to England. Sir George White comments:

'It is not generally known that some days before the investment of Ladysmith, Buller wired to me from Capetown asking me my intention. I said to hold on to Ladysmith. He replied that he thought I was right though the line of the Tugela river was tempting. The Boers had railways from the Orange Free State and from the Transvaal by two separate lines. While we held Ladysmith the Boers had to make the terminus of each of these lines some 5 to 7 miles North of Ladysmith. From these points ammunition and supplies had to be carried in wagons over rough ground, then distributed laterally not only to their positions round Ladysmith but also along their front on the Tugela. Had I fallen back it would have opened the railway to them as far as they could drive me. This would have been a great help to them in their advance to the south and later to their defence of the line of the Tugela.'

Mahan quotes the Prime Minister of Natal as saying that there had never been any suggestion of the abandonment or evacuation of Ladysmith. Sir George White writes:

'Local knowledge in Natal was too accurate as to the value of Ladysmith to Natal to admit of the idea of giving the town up to the enemy. I confidently appeal to the result. No Boer force of any considerable size crossed the Tugela'.

A mention by Mahan of the dangers of retreating in the face of an enemy greatly superior in mobility prompted Sir George White to comment as follows:

'If I had attempted to retreat south of Ladysmith the enemy would have been in Maritzburg before me. They could march 10 miles an hour – I could do 2½ to 3.'

The Commander-in-Chief, Lord Roberts, in a despatch to the Secretary of State for War dated 28 March 1900, wrote: 'Sir George White's decision to make a stand at Ladysmith was correct.'

Another book to appear in 1900 was of a totally different character. It was a highly critical study of the British Army's shortcomings as revealed in the first months of the war. The title 'An Absent-Minded War' was inspired by Rudyard Kipling's 'Absent-Minded Beggar', the happy-go-lucky British Tommy, and the author was an understandably anonymous 'British Officer.'

'It does not seem to have occurred to many people,' he wrote, 'that the epithet of "absent-minded" can be applied with equal correctness to Tommy's officers, from the highest to the lowest, and even to the Government at whose orders he has cheerfully marched to almost certain death on occasions without number.'

105

A few pages later, we read the following quotation from one of Buller's despatches:

'I suppose our officers will learn the value of scouting in time; but in spite of all one can say, up to this, our men seem to blunder into the midst of the enemy, and suffer accordingly.'

'And who,' asks the author, 'is more to blame for this than Sir Redvers Buller himself who, as Adjutant-General of the Army for several years, had every opportunity of seeing that our officers were being instructed on proper lines, and were being made to appreciate the importance of scouting and the best manner in which it should be performed? Did Sir Redvers Buller imagine that he could begin to instruct our officers in the rudiments of their profession when on the very battlefield itself? If he did think so, he has been cruelly undeceived.'

The German General Staff produced its own official History of the Boer War, and its author had difficulty in ascertaining what the British order of battle had been. In 1902 Colonel Rawlinson happened to be in Berlin and met the officer concerned.

'The fact was,' wrote Rawlinson in his diary, 'that we hadn't one; but the precise and orderly German mind could not conceive of a country going to war without a definite organization for its field army. My father was at the time editing our own official history, and I wrote to tell him of the difficulties of the Germans, and to suggest that it would be a friendly act to let them have "states" of our troops at various periods of the war. The Secretary of State for War saw no objection, the information was supplied, and the German General Staff was very grateful. I met the author after he had digested our returns, and his comment was:

"I know now why you took so long to beat the Boers".'

The Army's organisation came under close scrutiny by a Royal Commission, appointed in October, 1902 to investigate the military preparations for the war.

The use of naval guns, not only inside Ladysmith and by the relief column, but also in other battle areas, had attracted a great deal of public attention. On 13 February 1903 the proceedings at St Stephen's Hall, Westminster, were enlivened by pungent criticism of the performance of the Ladysmith guns by General Hunter. 'Our gun-laying in the Army,' he said, 'is infinitely better than the gun-laying in the Navy . . . I offered to take the girls out of school and serve the guns and make as good practice.'

It was certainly no coincidence that, during the ensuing fortnight of the hearings, eight senior Army officers who had seen naval guns in action on land in the war, were closely questioned about their range and accuracy.

Sir George White's evidence was heard first. 'The enemy fired over 10,000 yards into my position with Creusots', he said. 'If I had not telegraphed for those naval guns the moment I came up I should have had to fight the Boer guns with our field gun, which was a 15-pounder, the effective range of which was 3,500 yards; and when directed at an objective 4,000 yards off began to fall off rapidly . . . (the naval guns) kept the enemy's batteries a good way further off me than they otherwise would have been.'

Of the remaining seven officers, six praised the guns. A typical comment was: 'They were very accurate; the firing was very good indeed.' The eighth officer to give evidence on this matter had commanded a mobile column at the time and found the 12-pounders too cumbersome, though he described them as 'capital guns for infantry.'

General Hunter was on his own.

When asked to comment on Hunter's remarks, Hedworth Lambton, meanwhile promoted Rear-Admiral, told the Commissioners: 'General Hunter is a very brilliant man, but I do not suppose he had ever seen a big gun before, and he certainly knew nothing whatever about the shooting.'

Lambton and Hunter buried the hatchet later in the year. On 7 October the Press published an official statement emanating – curiously – from the Admiralty, quoting an apology from General Hunter for using 'expressions which he frankly admits should not have been used' and withdrawing them. The statement went on to say that Admiral Lambton, for his part, expressed his regret for the personal remarks made about General Hunter in his evidence before the Royal Commission. In fact, while Ladysmith was still under siege the War Office was taking the 4.7-in naval gun very seriously indeed. Four of these guns were fitted with field mounts in England and sent out to South Africa. These were in addition to the guns taken from warships in South Africa and adapted by Captain Percy Scott, who produced four different types of land mount for three types of gun.

The 4.7-in field gun was to remain in service into the First World War, until superseded by the new 6-in gun.

There was one area where the Royal Commission was able to apportion praise rather than blame. 'The transport by sea,' the Report stated, 'affords a remarkable illustration of what can be done when careful forethought and preparation is applied. If the same forethought had been applied throughout, there would have been little criticism to make with regard to the South African war.'

These transport arrangements were controlled by the Admiralty.

Lambton's evidence before the Royal Commission had important consequences for the technique of gunnery. Reynolds Sharp has mentioned how difficult it was to find the range at Ladysmith, nearly 4,000 feet above sea level, with guns designed for use at sea level. But there was more than just the difference of altitude to take into account. Lambton explained that the wide variations of temperature at Ladysmith during the South African summer, with cool nights and very hot days, affected the power of the cordite. As a result, the range varied by 500–600 yards between early morning and midday.

108

John Dreyer, a Captain of the Royal Artillery, who had served in South Africa (later Major-General, Director of Artillery, War Office, 1923–24) was impressed by Lambton's evidence and carried out a systematic investigation of all the variables affecting range: air density, wind, charge temperature and muzzle velocity. This led directly to the technique of 'calibration' which took all these factors into account and was adopted by the Royal Navy in 1905.

John was not the only member of his family to advance the science of gunnery. His brother, Admiral Sir Frederick Dreyer, was a disciple of Percy Scott and had been Flag Captain to Jellicoe at Jutland. They were sons of a Danish-born astronomer who had settled in Ireland.

Percy Scott himself was not called to give evidence before the Commission, though he was in England at the time. His name appears to have been mentioned only once during the proceedings, by Lambton. Admiral Harris was questioned at length about the guns sent ashore and studiously avoided any reference to the essential process of adaptation for land use and the officer who initiated it.

CHAPTER SEVEN
What Became of Them

I. REYNOLDS SHARP

THE transport *Columbian* brought *Powerful's* brigade to Simonstown, where they were given three cheers by their shipmates and the crews of *Doris* and *Niobe* and welcomed back on board. News came through that Captain Lambton had been made Commander of the Order of the Bath for his work in Ladysmith.

Powerful left Simonstown on 15 March and reached Portsmouth on 11 April. 'We came alongside the South Railway Jetty,' Sharp told me, 'and were given a tremendous reception. We were bidden to Windsor to be received by the Queen who gave us lunch and made us a little speech. I have always remembered her voice quite clearly as I stood very close to her because I was the last to be presented. Then, when we'd been presented, the Queen waved to our captain to bring the officers up again for her to speak to, which she did very graciously.

'A few days later we marched through London and were entertained at Lloyds. The men were presented with tobacco boxes and the officers with cigarette cases. It was very exciting to be received in such a friendly way.'

While Sharp was on his way to rejoin his ship at Simonstown for the passage home, Captain Percy Scott was winding up his affairs as Commandant of Durban prior to leaving for the Far East in *Terrible*. He found time to write a personal note in his own hand to my grandfather:

'Your son,' he wrote, 'has done very well at the front, and I am only sorry that his health broke down as I should have liked to have him in the ship.'

When *Powerful* returned to Portsmouth, one person par-
ticularly interested was the Vicar of Portsea, Cosmo Gordon
Lang, who had been Sharp's Divinity Tutor at Magdalen
College School, and was later to become Archbishop of
Canterbury. He wrote to my grandfather:

'Your son has certainly had an experience which few other men
in the Service have had, and it has come to him very early.'

It was indeed an experience which influenced Reynolds
Sharp for the rest of his life. Through contacts made at the
time in his own Service and in the Army, and kept up in later
years, notably by the annual reunion of the officers of the
Ladysmith garrison, he had a wide circle of friends, many of
whom had shared this experience, though not at such a
tender age.

After three months' rest and recuperation, Midshipman
Reynolds Sharp went to sea again on 14 July 1900, initially
in HMS *Resolution*, a battleship of the Channel Squadron. In
1904 he transferred to submarines. Later in the same year he
was specially promoted Lieutenant for service in South
Africa.

'I was one of a batch of six officers,' said Sharp, 'and we
were the third lot of submarine officers, so there would be
about a dozen fellows senior to me who were in submarines
before I was. They were all jolly good fellows and very
carefully selected. I was never so excited and thrilled as I was
with my appointment. I went down to Portsmouth and
joined up at the King's Stairs with a boat to take me off to the
submarine depot ship *Thames*, which was then moored up the
creek at Fareham with five Holland boats beside her. I was
told to go to Holland 2 which was one of five submarines
which were built at Barrow under licence from America.
They were very good sea boats and you could manoeuvre
them quite easily. Later on we had our own British-designed
boats, the A-boats.

'Normally we did our manoeuvring in Stokes Bay or Sandown
Bay but in the summer of 1904 my skipper Robert Ratcliff Cook

111

ventured out of the Channel, past Land's End and up to Milford Haven. Here we took part in night exercises. We used to lie on the surface, showing about a foot and a half of freeboard, and fire our torpedoes at the ships above us and claim a hit. That was the first time submarines went out of the English Channel.

'Later we took over Fort Blockhouse at the entrance to Portsmouth Harbour from the Army as our submarine depot. I went down to Plymouth for a year in command of A 10 – a devil of a boat – you had to have your hair parted in the middle to keep her afloat. Eventually in 1907 I was fortunate enough to get command of C 2, a magnificent boat.'

Those were the early days of motoring and Sharp owned a succession of cars, his favourite being a single-cylinder Renault. He used to say that he had broken down at every milestone on the Portsmouth Road. His interest in things mechanical extended to aircraft, which were much in the news at that time with the first powered flight in England and Blériot's Channel crossing.

Sharp and a fellow submarine-commander Alfred Prowse, who had his own aeroplane, applied for permission to take up flying in the Service. They were interviewed at the Admiralty by the Second Sea Lord's Naval Assistant, Captain Robert Falcon Scott. Scott had returned to the Navy after his Antarctic expedition in *Discovery* (1901–03) and was planning his next expedition, which was to end so tragically.

But the would-be naval aviators were before their time. Scott told them that the Navy did not intend to have any heavier-than-air machines; they might have a few balloons, he said. So back they went to submarines.

Promoted to Lieut.-Commander in 1911, Sharp was Commander Instructor to the Royal Naval Reserve in Bristol from 1912 to 1914. From the latter year until his retirement in 1922 he was stationed at Berehaven, Ireland. During the war he combined the duties of Chief Examination Officer, King's Harbour Master and Coaling Officer.

His work included salvaging ships torpedoed by U-boats and checking cargoes of enemy and neutral merchant ship-

112

ping intercepted by the Navy. When the Americans came into the war, part of the US battle fleet was based in Bantry Bay, including the flagship *Utah* and the battleships *Nevada* and *Oklahoma*.

Reynolds Sharp, then Acting Commander, carried out liaison work with the Americans and personally piloted the flagship into harbour. He lived at Waterfall Cottage, opposite Bere Island, a few miles from his office at Castletownbere and kept open house for the officers of both navies.

Typical entries in the Berehaven Coastguard log during the war were:

20 October 1914: Sailing ship *Ulrich*, German prize, 2,201 tons, 3,800 tons of nitrate, piloted, berthed and took charge.

14 August 1915: Sailing ship *Baltzer*, 343 tons, cargo timber, bottom up, assisted in and moored, masts had to be broken off to enable her to be brought in.

10 January 1917: SS *Alexandrian*, 4,467 tons, 6,000 tons general cargo, had been torpedoed and sinking, piloted her, had to beach her in NW gale, shifted her on 24.3.17 and beached in Mill Cove. All Examination vessels assisting.

6 April 1917: SS Hundvaago, Norwegian steamer, 1,124 tons, cargo 1,600 tons ground nuts, torpedoed, rudder and propeller gone. King's Harbour Master beached her, tugs *Sportsman*, *Drake*, and *Reindeer* attending. Repaired locally. Left 28.7.17 for Liverpool in tow of *Herculaneum* and *Hornby*.

At the end of a list of ships handled in the period from October 1914 to May 1918, there is the following footnote:

'2,500 survivors landed, about one-half were brought in by Examination vessels.'

Berehaven is a small harbour inside Bantry Bay, well sheltered from the south-west by Bere Island. The rest of Bantry Bay is open to the Atlantic. Those who have lived in the area, or have been to sea in small craft in the western approaches in bad weather, will best be able to appreciate the conditions under which the staff of the Berehaven Harbour Master had to work in wartime.

113

'Berehaven, you may think,' said Sharp, 'is the last place in the world, but that wasn't what Napoleon himself thought about it. He knew that the South of Ireland was the key to the supply of the British Navy and the Army, which might be in France, as indeed it turned out. When he was on St Helena, I understand that he said that the mistake of his life was to have gone to Egypt instead of Ireland.'

After the war came the Irish 'troubles.' Reynolds Sharp continued his work in Berehaven, which remained a British Naval base for a number of years after the establishment of the Irish Free State, until his retirement in 1922. Difficult times though they were for a British officer, he was on friendly terms with the local population, including the Roman Catholic and Protestant clergy. 'I was very warmly received by the people,' he told me. 'Many of them were very good friends of mine and have been for years afterwards.'

Half a century after Reynolds Sharp left Berehaven, there are still people in those parts who remember him with affection.

Retiring with the rank of Commander, Reynolds Sharp became an active member of a committee of Earl Haig's Officers Association, engaged in placing ex-servicemen in civilian employment.

In the mid-1930s, he took over as Secretary of the Ladysmith Dinner Club, which organized an annual reunion on the anniversary of the relief, 28 February.

'When we were in Ladysmith,' Sharp told me, 'we officers decided that if we got out, we'd have a jolly good dinner every year. For many years the dinner was organised by Martin Archer-Shee, who was in the Gloucestershire Regiment in the First War, and incidentally started his service career as a Midshipman. The dinner was just for ourselves, though we did invite the Press, as there had been several important journalists in Ladysmith. The Prince of Wales dined with us in 1932 and Lord Athlone, who had fought in the Boer War himself and later been Governor General of the Union, in 1937.

114

'One day I met Sir Hubert Gough in Pall Mall, and he said:

"Look here, I understand you're having a dinner in a week or two: I should like to come." I said: "You're not entitled!" "Why not?" he asked. "You weren't in Ladysmith, you were outside, you were relieving us". "Yes," he said, "but I was inside as well." "You couldn't be inside as well as outside, how could you be?" "Oh, yes," he said, "I was because I got in the day before with Lord Dundonald's force." "Well," I said, "in that case I'll see what I can do." And, bless his heart, he came to our dinner, we all loved him very much, and he came again another year.

'After Martin Archer-Shee died in 1935 I took on the job of Secretary, being the youngest surviving officer of the garrison, and we kept the dinner going until 1951, by which time we were getting too old to assemble in London in midwinter. So we met together for 50 years, and I believe that was much longer than the Waterloo dinner.'

In 1939 Reynolds Sharp offered his services again, and was employed in Naval Control work in Weymouth and Stockholm. He died in 1966 in his eighty-third year.

II   EDWARD CHICHESTER

Edward Chichester, alas, missed HMS *Powerful's* triumphal return to Portsmouth, the royal reception at Windsor and the march through London. We next find him writing home to his mother from Capetown on 21 March. 'I am getting much better and am putting on flesh fast. Dad says I can shoot rooks all day long, also may ride his horse.'

He came home in the liner *Orotava* and in due course returned to duty in *Magnificent*. In 1904 he too was especially promoted Lieutenant. From 1905 to 1906 he was Flag Lieutenant to the Senior Naval Officer, Gibraltar, a post then held by his father. On the latter's death in 1906 he succeeded to the baronetcy.

He was promoted Lieut.-Commander in 1915, and in that year served at Larne, Northern Ireland, a post as important as Berehaven in the battle against the U-boats. His next posting was to the staff of the Commander-in-Chief, Coast of Scotland, stationed at Rosyth.

Retiring from the Service after the war with the rank of Commander, he went into business and was a director of the Wallsend Slipway and Engineering Company. He rejoined the Navy in 1939 and worked in the Trade Division of the Admiralty, his office being in the underground 'citadel' in Whitehall. He died in September, 1940.

III IAN FORBES

ON 14 March the Gordons left Ladysmith for Arcadia Camp, 7½ miles out on the road to Van Reenen's Pass. Conditions there, as the camp's name implied, were a great improvement on Ladysmith. 'The air here,' Forbes wrote, 'is splendid. The camp lies between two spruits on very rocky ground. We get fresh milk and butter daily.'

Beside drill and field exercises there were opportunities to visit the battlefields of the Tugela Front. On 18 March Frobes went up Spion Kop.

'The place where the infantry went up is quite wonderful, being only a path up a shoulder. The front is a precipice. But having got there I cannot understand why they went away. On top there are rows of graves marked with rough crosses – great long trenches. The Boer graves are dotted about down at the foot.'

Forbes was constantly feeling unwell. On 22 March he obtained a fortnight's leave and went down to Durban. He was examined by Dr Brodie on board the hospital ship *Lismore Castle* and found to be suffering from mild enteric as a result of starvation and bad food. After the fever left him he got jaundice and in his own words 'wasted away to a shadow.' By the middle of April he had recovered sufficiently to travel, and was granted four months' home leave. On 19 April he left Durban for the Cape, via Simonstown where the empty cartridge cases from the Naval guns fired in and around Ladysmith were offloaded from his ship.

Of the port he wrote:

'Simonstown is a quaint little place, a big camp for Boer prisoners, a few houses and the *Monarch*, *Pelorous* and *Doris* lying alongside.'

At Capetown he transferred to the *Kildonan Castle* for the homeward trip. Of Table Bay he wrote:

'Such a curious sight to see the crowds of transports that are in the bay, some empty, some full of troops, some with horses, forage, stores etc. There are 198 ships employed.'

The 10,000 ton *Kildonan Castle* was brand new and after launching had been fitted out in 16 days by gangs of 2,000 men working round the clock. Such was the need for troop transports that the ship went straight into service without the customary trials. 'The Company,' wrote Forbes, 'is clearing about £8,000 – 9,000 per month from the Government. It costs about £9,000 to run and the Government pay £17,000.'

On the homeward voyage numerous transports were sighted on their way to the Cape: on 11 May alone five ships passed nearby. On board ship Forbes was gratified to find some of his own photographs of Ladysmith reproduced in the magazine 'Navy & Army Illustrated.'

He reached Southampton on 14 May and after a night in London took the sleeper from King's Cross to Huntly. Back home at Rothiemay on 16 May he changed into the kilt, went down to the local Hall, escorted by a guard of honour, spoke for an hour on his experiences and was played back home by the pipers.

Forbes was examined by the local doctor, who told him that he must be very careful as he had a weak heart.

His Ladysmith diary ends with the following entry:

'*19 May*: On account of the relief of Mafeking the scholars came round with flags and drums, etc. At 10 pm we had fireworks on the bridge and they made a great show. I was asked to set off the first one and in the end returned thanks for the way they cheered me.'

After recuperating at home, Forbes was Adjutant at the Depot in Aberdeen.

In 1902 he served on the staff of Lord Cadogan, the Lord Lieutenant of Ireland, and in the following year became Adjutant of Volunteers (Lanarkshire Rifles) in Glasgow. In 1912 he transferred to the Royal Scots Fusiliers.

In their invasion of Belgium in August, 1914, the Germans succeeded within three weeks in occupying Brussels and capturing Liege and Namur. But Antwerp continued to hold out, and largely as a result of this resistance all the French and Belgian Channel ports and their hinterland remained for the time being in Allied hands.

At the end of September, when German heavy artillery was pounding the forts of Antwerp, the Belgian Government, which had moved there from Brussels, appealed to Britain for assistance. As the British Expeditionary Force was engaged elsewhere, help was sent direct from Britain. The forces included the 7th Division under Major-General Capper, which landed at Zeebrugge on 6 October. The division included a battalion of the Royal Scots Fusiliers commanded by Major Ian Forbes.

This division and the 3rd Cavalry Division, also sent direct to Belgium from Britain, came under the orders of General Rawlinson, whom we last encountered in Ladysmith. Rawlinson had up to that time been in command of the 4th Division of the British Expeditionary Force on the Aisne, due at this juncture to be transferred to Flanders.

But the two fresh divisions from England were too late to save Antwerp. As the 7th marched through Bruges the day after landing, news of the imminent surrender of Antwerp reached them and the streams of refugees from the East told their own story. In fact, at about the time the division had been disembarking, the Germans were crossing the Schelde river above Antwerp, forcing the Belgian Army to retreat westwards to avoid being cut off.

On 13 October Rawlinson was ordered to move on Ypres, so the next day the first units of the British Army, now designated the IVth Corps, set out for the town which was to pass into British military history. General Capper was ordered to a line of villages east of Ypres. Forbes's battalion was in Poezelhoek 6 miles from the town, just off the main road from Ypres to Menin, which was known to be occupied by the Germans. Forbes's diary again takes up the story:

'*Poezelhoek, 16 October*: The Germans were quite close to us here, and from three in the morning there was heavy firing. We marched at 4.00 through bitter cold of the dawn and took up our position in a chateau which had not yet been touched. There were really beautiful grounds with positive hedges of geraniums and chrysanthemums and hydrangeas, orchards with trees laden with fruit, greenhouses full of cuttings for next year. We were there ten days and saw the whole place gradually ruined. Trenches had to be dug across the lawns and flower beds, and shells soon battered down the pretty house and spoilt the lovely grounds, most heartrending to see. It was not our fault; we were most careful to spoil as little as we could. When we dug trenches through a flowerbed, we replanted the flowers as neatly as possible, or through a lawn, we replaced the turf, or through a path the gravel. I cleared the greenhouses most carefully to make a sleeping-place for my men because I did not want to take the carriages out of the coach-house to be spoilt by the rain; I did not foresee that a German shell would come and shatter them all to atoms.

'The chateau was so prettily furnished, left just as it was when the owners fled, with silk damask on the walls, china in cabinets, a polished table in the dining-room, and everything nice that well-off people of taste would have in their house; and it was all battered down into a heap of bricks and mortar.'

Within two days the battalion found itself under almost continuous fire.

'It is very difficult from this time on to differentiate between day and night. With only occasional lulls, the terrific din of firing went on without ceasing and there was no question of getting a night's sleep; shells, guns, and rifles all going at once made one's recollections of the Boer fire seem like crackers let off at a picnic. And all the time the Boches coming on, rows on rows of cannon fodder;

119

four or five to one perhaps more, they were, but as we were in good trenches we had only slight losses at first.'

Sir Frederick Maurice, in his 'Life of General Lord Rawlinson', describes this stage of the battle from the Army Commander's point of view:

'With his troops locked fast in the front, at the head of the Ypres salient, where they had to bear the brunt of the German storm, no manoeuvre was possible, and there was not much for Rawlinson to do, save to watch the gallant fight of his 7th Division. He felt keenly that his men were being asked to do too much, and said so in a report to GHQ.'

The biographer then quotes Rawlinson's diary:

'On the 24th the Germans penetrated the line near Poezelhoek, and succeeded as far as I can ascertain in scuppering most of the Wiltshire Regiment. We are only hanging on by our eyelids, our losses in the last two days have been 100 officers and 2,000 men, exclusive of the Wiltshire Regiment.'

Forbes wrote:

'Our D Company trenches having had to be abandoned on Trafalgar and Elandslaagte Day (21 October) – which ought to have brought us better luck – we were ordered to retake them at dusk on the following day. The trenches were in a village, and at first all went well, though it was nervous work in the dark approaching houses concealing snipers. The first few were easily captured . . . I went up to the centre house of the village – a large one from which the Germans were pouring incessant fire, and shouted to the occupants to surrender, as they were surrounded. They threw their rifles out of the window and came out of the door, forming up in front of the house with meticulous precision. I walked along their line flashing my torch at them to see how many there were, when I noticed that the left man of the rear section of fours, an immense burly brute, still had his rifle in his hand. I took hold of it when he muttered something in German, drew it back, placed it against my stomach and fired. Luckily, my instinct was as quick or quicker than his action, and I pushed the rifle down so that the bullet went between my legs. Then all was confusion.

Corporal Reid of my Company, who was standing by me, at once shot the man in the back of the head and also stuck his bayonet into him when on the ground to make sure of him – (Reid afterwards got the DCM and was killed at Festubert) – and there was firing in every direction, in the midst of which I discovered that a whole German regiment was coming up behind the house. I had no alternative but to retreat.'

For the action just described, Forbes was awarded the DSO.

In the twelve days following its arrival in the area, Forbes's battalion was reduced in strength from 1,000 to 500 men, and by the end of the month the Division itself had lost all but 3,000 of its 18,000 men.

On the 28th Forbes was wounded in the chest and invalided home. But seven weeks later he was back in Flanders, to find the Army bogged down after the inconclusive end of the first Battle of Ypres.

'*Westoutre, 18 December*. Everything here is very miserable and in a sea of mud. I was not encouraged by being received with "What a b—— fool you are to have come back!" I began to think I was, all the circumstances considered.

'*Trenches, 1 January*. The trench was absolutely awful. We could not dig anywhere for the poor dead French soldiers. They have never been buried, and now are just trodden into the mud. The mud and water, as usual, took me over my knees most of the way and over my waist the rest. The cold was intense; there was no dug-out for the officers and we were under fire all the time. After I made the dug-out behind the trench, I was not so badly off, for I got a brazier of coke and got my clothes a bit dryer. How the men stick it out, I do not know. They are really splendid.'

In the last week of January Forbes was in constant pain and felt sick. Appendicitis was diagnosed and he was ordered home.

After recovering from his operation in Charing Cross Hospital, he got command of the Training battalion at Fort Matilda, Greenock, where he remained till 1919.

He retired from the Army in 1921, but continued to take a

great interest in the Territorials, and was for a period Hon. Colonel of the 6th Gordons, the local Territorial Battalion. He died in 1957.

IV THE SENIOR OFFICERS

AT the 'khaki' General Election of October, 1900, Hedworth Lambton stood unsuccessfully as a Liberal in Newcastle-upon-Tyne. He then successively commanded the Royal Yacht *Victoria & Albert*; was promoted Rear-Admiral (October 1902); spent a year as Second-in-Command to Lord Charles Beresford in the Channel Fleet; commanded the cruiser division in the Mediterranean; and was Vice-Admiral and Commander-in-Chief in China.

In December, 1910 he inherited a fortune from the widow of Sir Henry Meux, 3rd Baronet, and changed his name to Meux the following year by Royal licence. This unusual turn of events was the final episode in a story that began during the siege of Ladysmith. Lady Meux heard of the exploits of the Naval 12-pr guns used by Captain Lambton's brigade and personally ordered a battery of six similar guns to be manufactured at Armstrong's Elswick works at Newcastle. She presented the guns to Lord Roberts for use in South Africa, where they were known as the 'Elswick' battery and manned by the 1st Northumberland Volunteer Artillery. On his return to England in 1900 after the siege, Captain Lambton visited Lady Meux and thanked her for her patriotic gesture. She subsequently changed her Will, naming him her heir, provided that he took the name of her late husband.

Hedworth Meux was promoted Admiral in 1911 and, after a period on half pay, was Commander-in-Chief at Portsmouth from 1912 to 1916. On the outbreak of war he was responsible for the safe transport of the British Expeditionary Force to France.

In 1915 he was promoted Admiral of the Fleet. In 1916 he entered parliament unopposed as Conservative member for Portsmouth when the seat fell vacant on the elevation of Lord Charles Beresford to the peerage. He retired from parliament at the General Election of 1918. In the words of Reynolds Sharp, Hedworth Meux was 'a man tremendously respected and very powerful politically.' He died in 1929.

Percy Scott remained on the China Station for two years in command of HMS *Terrible* and finally brought the cruiser home to pay off in September, 1902. The following year he was appointed to command HMS *Excellent*, the Naval Gunnery School at Portsmouth. In 1905 he was promoted Rear-Admiral and Inspector of Target Practice to introduce rapid, accurate and long-distance fire and bring some uniformity to gunnery methods throughout the Service.

In 1907 he commanded the 2nd Cruiser Squadron of the Home Fleet under Admiral Lord Charles Beresford at the height of the latter's quarrel with the First Sea Lord, Admiral Sir John Fisher. Scott, being a loyal supporter of Fisher and his reforms was drawn into the quarrel, and there were a number of unfortunate incidents between him and Beresford which were sensationalised in the Press and caused debate in Parliament over the 'disunion' between senior naval officers. As a result, Scott was placed in command of a special service squadron to visit South Africa and South America. In fact, he was sent as far away from home waters as possible, and after that he was never employed again on the active list.

He resigned from the Service in 1913 at a time when he was under attack in the popular Press. His interest in gunnery continued during his retirement as also his co-operation with Messrs. Vickers on his most important single contribution to naval gunnery: a system of centralised fire control known as director firing, the gun director being sited in the foretop and all guns of the broadside being laid and trained to correspond with the director.

When the war came he was much in demand as adviser on gunnery matters, and he created the Anti Aircraft Corps for the defence of London against Zeppelin attack.

Scott's day was the heyday of the battleship. Master gunner though he was, he foresaw sooner than most people that these enormously expensive capital ships would be vulnerable to air and submarine attack. When in 1922 the House of Commons was debating the Defence Estimates, he described the proposed construction of two battleships as 'a wicked waste of taxpayers' money.' 'The Royal Navy,' he went on, 'is no longer our first line of defence and offence. The Air is!'

Admiral Sir Percy Scott, 1st Baronet, died in 1924. I am indebted to his biographer for the following appraisal: 'He was not only the greatest naval gunner, probably of any age, as his career coincided with the revolution in ordnance which made modern accurate gunnery possible, but also perhaps the most prescient of British naval prophets – and not honoured in his own country.'

Scott's prophecies on air and submarine power have since been only too convincingly fulfilled. The Japanese were the first to demonstrate what air power can do against warships; and today's capital ship is the nuclear submarine.

In their accounts of the siege, Reynolds Sharp, Ian Forbes and Sir George White mention a number of their colleagues of the garrison, and others engaged in the fighting elsewhere. Among them were many who distinguished themselves at the time or later. Some became national figures and the details of their later careers will be familiar to many. Their involvement in that war of long ago is perhaps less well known.

Lieutenant-Colonel Sir Martin Archer-Shee (1873-1935) Lieutenant and Adjutant, 19th Hussars in Ladysmith, won the DSO in the Boer War. In the First World War he commanded the 12th battalion of the Gloucestershire Regiment from 1915 to 1917; then the 2-4 York & Lancasters and the King's Own Scottish Borderers. He was Unionist Member of Parliament for Finsbury from 1910 to 1923.

Major-General Sir Geoffrey Barton (1844-1922) commanded the 6th Brigade of the Natal Field Force in the advance on Ladysmith. He was wounded at the Battle of Pieters Hill on 27 February, 1900.

General Sir Redvers Buller, V.C. (1839-1908) commanded the reorganised Natal Field Force after the relief of Ladysmith. His advance through Northern Natal to the Transvaal frontier took from May to August, 1900. His forces then formed the right flank of the British offensive in the Eastern Transvaal towards Portuguese East Africa.

Buller returned home in November, 1900 and was appointed to the Aldershot Command. At a regimental luncheon in October the following year he attacked the 'Times' newspaper for asserting that he was not fit to be in command of the First Army Corps, and launched into a diatribe about his 'surrender' telegram which, though still unpublished, had been referred to in that newspaper. It was the end for Buller. He was relieved of his command and placed on half pay. In spite of his professional downfall, Buller's status as a national hero was unaffected. A distinguished serving soldier and military historian who, like Buller, comes from the West Country, has told the author: "Even in the thirties, when I was a boy, Buller was still greatly honoured, his reputation not at all diminished by the aspersions of outsiders".

General Sir Beauchamp Duff (1855-1918), Colonel on Ladysmith HQ Staff had come, like most of the forces that landed in Natal at the beginning of the war, from India. He returned there and became successively Adjutant-General, Chief of Staff, and from 1913 to 1916, Commander-in-Chief.

The Earl of Dundonald (1852-1935), whose flying column was the first unit to enter Ladysmith at the relief, commanded the Canadian Militia from 1902 to 1904 and served overseas in the First World War. In 1921 he was special Ambassador to the Peruvian Centenary celebrations. This assignment recalled the part which his grandfather, Lord Cochrane, had played in assisting both Peru and Chile to win their independence from Spain.

Major-General Sir William Gatacre (1843-1906) commanded the 3rd Division of the South African Field Force from the start of the war until May, 1900. On 10 December, 1899, when operating to the south of the Orange River which formed the border with Cape Colony, he suffered a severe reverse at Stormberg. This defeat was the first of three events in the course of what became known as 'Black Week,' the others taking place at Colenso, as already described, and Magersfontein (see Methuen, below).

General Sir Hubert Gough (1870 – 1963), Captain 16th Lancers, Intelligence Officer to Lord Dundonald's mounted brigade in South Africa, was professor at the Staff College from 1904 to 1906 and commanded the 16th Lancers from 1907 to 1911. At the start of the First World War he went out to Belgium in command of the 3rd Cavalry Brigade. He served continuously on the Western front and rose to command the Fifth Army – the youngest General in the field at the time. This Army, under strength and lacking adequate reinforcement at the material time, bore the full brunt of the massive enemy offensive which carried the Germans forward some 40 miles, to within a short distance of Amiens in March/April, 1918. Gough was made the scapegoat for his Army's forced retreat and relieved of his command after the first week's fighting. Nearly twenty years were to pass before his action, and consequently the honour of the Fifth Army, which had been popularly supposed to have "run away", were vindicated.

"Goughie", as he was known to his friends, went into business between the wars, and one of his positions was Chairman of Siemens Bros. In the Second World War he served in the Home Guard until at age 72, he was asked to retire.

Admiral Sir Lionel Halsey (1872-1949), a Lieutenant in HMS *Powerful's* Naval brigade in Ladysmith, saw action in the First World War in the Heligoland Bight, at the Dogger Bank and at Jutland. He commanded the Royal Australian Navy from 1918 to 1920 and was Comptroller and Treasurer to the Prince of Wales from 1920 to 1936.

General Sir Ian Hamilton (1855-1947), Colonel on the Ladysmith Staff, commanded a mounted infantry division during the advance from Bloemfontein to Pretoria and into

126

the eastern Transvaal. After a spell at the War Office, he returned to South Africa in the later stages of the war as Chief of Staff to Lord Kitchener. In 1910 he was appointed Commander-in-Chief in the Mediterranean and Inspector-General of Overseas Forces.

On the outbreak of war in 1914 he was made Commander-in-Chief of the Home Defence Army. In 1915 he commanded the Expeditionary Force which attempted to force the Dardanelles. By the autumn of that year stalemate had been reached, and Hamilton recommended withdrawal from the Gallipoli peninsula – a course which was ultimately adopted. He was thereupon recalled and replaced by Sir C. Munro.

Hamilton was recommended for the VC after the battle of Elandslaagte, Natal, in October, 1899, but was considered too senior to receive the award. In his earlier career he had commanded a platoon of the Gordons at Majuba Hill in 1881.

Lieut.-General Sir Archibald Hunter (1856-1936) commanded the 10th Division in South Africa in 1900. His subsequent commands were: Scotland 1902-03; Western Army Corps, then Southern Army, India 1904-09; Gibraltar 1910-13; 13th Western Division, UK 1914; and 3rd Army, 1914. From 1918 to 1922 he was Conservative and Unionist member of Parliament for Lancaster.

General Sir Nevil Macready (1862-1946), Major with the Gordons in Ladysmith, had been commissioned into the Regiment in 1881 and served with them in Egypt. After the relief of Ladysmith he saw further action in the Transvaal. After the war he was for three years Chief Staff Officer in Cape Colony. In April, 1914 he was General Officer Commanding, Belfast, at the time of the unrest over Irish Home Rule. On the outbreak of war in 1914 he became Adjutant-General to the British Expeditionary Force. From 1920 to 1922 he was Commander-in-Chief in Ireland, the last British officer to hold that post.

Field-Marshal Lord Methuen (1845-1932) was Major-

General in command of the 3rd Division of the 1st Army Corps charged with the task of relieving Kimberley, Methuen was defeated at Magersfontein on 11 December 1899, in the 'Black Week' already referred to in an earlier chapter. His service in South Africa continued into the guerrilla war phase, and he returned there in the capacity of Commander-in-Chief from 1908 to 1912.

General Lord Rawlinson (1864-1925), Lieutenant-Colonel Sir H. Rawlinson on Ladysmith HQ Staff, joined Lord Roberts's HQ at Bloemfontein at the end of March 1900, and worked on the organisation of the army for the advance on Pretoria. After a short spell at home, he returned to South Africa in 1901 and commanded a mobile column engaged in rounding up Boer guerrillas. From 1903 to 1906 he was Commandant of the Staff College.

In the early years of the First World War he commanded the 4th Division of the British Expeditionary Force, then the 4th Army itself. In 1918 he was British Military Representative on the Supreme War Council. In 1919 he carried out the evacuation of the Allied Forces in North Russia. From 1920 till his death in Delhi in 1925 he was Commander-in-Chief, India.

Sir Edward Ward, Bart, (1853-1925), responsible for food supplies in Ladysmith, was Permanent Under-Secretary for War from 1901 to 1914 and chairman of the Commission which set up the Officers Training Corps.

The Earl of Ypres (1852-1925), General French in South Africa, who had left Ladysmith in the last train to get out before the siege and had later relieved Kimberley, was Chief of the Imperial General Staff from 1911 to 1914; Commander-in-Chief of the British Expeditionary Force in France 1914-1915; Commander-in-Chief Home Forces from 1916; and Lord Lieutenant of Ireland from 1918 to 1921.

CHAPTER EIGHT

Chronology

TO JUNE 5 1900

1895 May
27 *Terrible* launched at Clydebank.
July
24 *Powerful* launched at Barrow.
December
29 Dr Jameson starts abortive Raid on Johannesburg.

1897 June
8 *Powerful* commissioned at Portsmouth.
26 *Terrible* and *Powerful* present at Queen Victoria's Jubilee Naval Review.
October
8 *Powerful* leaves for China Station.

1898 March
24 *Terrible* commissioned at Portsmouth.

1899 May
25 Sir A. Milner declares that if Natal is invaded, the Colony will be defended 'by the whole force of the Empire.'
May 31-June
5 Bloemfontein Conference (Milner/Kruger).
August
9 Joseph Chamberlain, British Colonial Secretary, announces decision to send military reinforcements to Natal.
Cadet Reynolds Sharp passes out from *Britannia* at Dartmouth; wins prizes for seamanship, charts and instruments, and boat sailing.

September

4   *Powerful* leaves Yokohama for home waters.

8   Government sanction given for despatch of reinforcements to South Africa from India, Britain and the Mediterranean: total 20,662 officers and men.

11   Lieutenant-General Sir George White appointed to command Natal Field Force.

13   Major-General Sir A. Hunter appointed Chief of Staff in Natal.

16   White and his staff leave for South Africa.

17   *Powerful* leaves Hong Kong.

18   Admiralty orders *Powerful* and *Terrible* to proceed via the Cape instead of Suez.

2nd Bn the Gordon Highlanders leave Ambala for Natal.

Sharp joins *Terrible* at Portsmouth for passage to China Station.

19   *Terrible* sails from Portsmouth.

21   *Powerful* arrives at Singapore.

23   Lieutenant-General J.D.P. French and Major D. Haig leave Southampton for South Africa.

25   *Terrible* coals at Las Palmas, Canary Islands.

26   Force of all arms leaves Ladysmith for Glencoe Junction.

28   Natal Government calls out Volunteer Corps.

October

2   First transport arrives at Durban from India with reinforcements.

President Kruger of the Transvaal declares that war is inevitable.

3   *Powerful* calls at Mauritius and embarks 4 co's 2nd Battalion, King's Own Yorkshire Light Infantry.

White arrives at Capetown.

7   *Terrible* calls at St. Helena.

White lands at Durban.

9   Boer Ultimatum

General Sir Redvers Buller, VC appointed

Commander-in-Chief 1st Army Corps (i.e. forces in South Africa).

Lieutenant Ian Forbes, Gordon Highlanders, arrives at Durban from India with 2nd Battalion.

White meets Governor of Natal.

10 *Powerful* calls at Durban but does not land troops.

Gordons arrive at Ladysmith.

General French and Major Haig arrive at Capetown.

11 Boer ultimatum expires; state of war.

12 British agent leaves Pretoria.

Boer invasion of Natal.

1st Bn Royal Irish Fusiliers arrives at Durban.

13 *Powerful* lands Koyli's at Capetown and proceeds to Simonstown for rendezvous with *Terrible*.

14 *Terrible* arrives at Simonstown.

Buller sails from Southampton. Also on board: Winston Churchill and W.K.L. Dickson and his 'Biograph' cine-camera team.

15 Reynolds Sharp rated Midshipman.

16 Kimberley and Mafeking invested.

20 First Naval Brigade landed in South Africa.

Battle of Talana Hill, Glencoe, Natal.

French and Haig arrive at Ladysmith.

21 Captain Scott's improvised land mountings for four long-range Naval 12-pounder guns ready in Simonstown dockyard.

Battle of Elandslaagte, Natal.

23 Martial law declared in Natal.

25 Telegram received at Simonstown from White in Ladysmith asking for Naval personnel and guns.

26 Land mountings for two 4.7-in Naval guns ready at Simonstown.

Sharp and Chichester transfer from *Terrible* to *Powerful*.

Powerful sails for Durban with guns for Ladysmith.

29 *Powerful* arrives at Durban. Naval Brigade disembarks and leaves for Ladysmith.

30 Naval Brigade arrives and immediately goes into action

131

in 'battle of Ladysmith.'

Disaster at Nicholson's Nek.

31 Buller arrives at Capetown.

November

2 Ladysmith besieged.

French and Haig leave Ladysmith in last train out.

3 Ladysmith cavalry reconnaissance towards Lancer's Hill.

Terrible leaves Simonstown for Durban.

5 Intombi hospital camp established outside Ladysmith by agreement between combatants.

6 *Terrible* arrives at Durban.

7 Scott appointed Commandant of Durban.

Naval Brigade landed from *Terrible*.

8 Naval guns set up for land defence of Durban.

6-in Creusot gun on Bulwana Hill starts shelling Ladysmith.

9 Boer attack on Ladysmith: Garrison fires 21-gun salute with live ammunition in honour of Prince of Wales's birthday.

14 Ladysmith garrison reconnaissance to Rifleman's Ridge.

15 Armoured train disaster near Colenso: Winston Churchill captured by Boers.

17-
22 Transports arrive at Capetown with 22,000 troops.

22 Buller leaves Capetown for Durban (arrives Durban 25).

24 Ladysmith loses 228 head of oxen to Boers.

25 Communication with Ladysmith established by searchlight from Estcourt.

Battle of Graspan (Enslin).

26 First issue of 'Ladysmith Lyre' news-sheet published.

27 Naval Brigade from *Terrible* leaves Durban to join Buller's force at Frere.

30 Heavy bombardment of Ladysmith.

December

1   6-in Boer gun starts firing from Gun Hill.

2   Casualties among wounded in town hospital.

7   Heliograph two-way communication with Ladysmith established from Weenen.

7-
8   Sortie from Ladysmith under General Hunter destroys two Boer guns on Gun Hill.

11 Sortie by 2nd Battalion, Rifle Brigade destroys 4-in howitzer on Surprise Hill.

10-
16 'Black Week': British reverses at Stormberg, Magersfontein & Colenso.

13 Reynolds Sharp admitted to Intombi hospital with dysentery.
    Terrible's Naval Brigade goes into action against Boer positions at Colenso.

15 Battle of Colenso.

18 Field-Marshal Lord Roberts appointed C in C, South Africa: General Lord Kitchener his C of S.

21 White's Ladysmith HQ bombed out.

23 Roberts sails for South Africa.
    Winston Churchill lands at Durban after escaping from Boer captivity.

1900 January

6   Major Boer attack on Ladysmith: 17 hours' continuous fighting.

8   British forces south of Tugela river total 30,000 men.

10 Roberts and Kitchener arrive at Capetown.

11 Buller crossed Tugela at Potgieter's Drift.

18 Successful cavalry action by Lord Dundonald west of Acton Homes.

23-
27 Battle of Spion Kop. Heavy British casualties, followed by withdrawal across Tugela river.

27 Peak of fever cases in Ladysmith: 1,314. Daily death rate averages 8.

31 Naval Brigade ('Grant's Guns') landed at Port Elizabeth.

 2 'Chevril' horse extract issued in Ladysmith. Bread ration: ½-lb daily.
 5 Buller starts attempt to relieve Ladysmith via Vaal Krantz.
 7 British retreat from Vaal Krantz.
    Boer 'Long Tom' gun, transferred from Ladysmith, starts bombarding Kimberley.
10 Buller and main force of Natal Army return to Chieveley.
11 Reynolds Sharp discharged from hospital.
12 Boers start attempt to dam Klip river, Ladysmith.
15 Kimberley relieved by General French.
17 Buller attacks Monte Cristo.
19 Buller drives Boers from Hlangwane Hill, near Colenso.
20 Colenso occupied.
21 Buller's forces cross Tugela river.
22 Attack on Boer positions north of Colenso, which continues for three days.
    Ladysmith bread ration increased to 1 lb per day.
27 Ladysmith bread ration reduced to ½-lb per day.
    Battle of Pieter's Hill, Colenso.
    Cronje surrenders to Roberts at Paardeberg.
28 Lord Dundonald's Flying Column enters Ladysmith; siege raised.

March
 1 Buller enters Ladysmith.
 3 Ceremonial entry of Relief Force.
    Total British casualties on all fronts to date: killed, wounded, missing and prisoners: 885 officers and 11,892 men.
 5 Presidents of the Boer Republics make overtures of peace.
 7 Naval Brigade leaves Ladysmith.

9 White leaves Ladysmith.

11 Lord Salisbury replies to Boer peace overtures.

12 *Powerful*'s Naval Brigade arrives at Simonstown on board transport *Columbian*.

13 Occupation of Bloemfontein.

14 Scott relinquishes duties as Commandant of Durban.

15 *Powerful* leaves Simonstown for UK.

23 Lieutenant Ian Forbes, the Gordons, arrives at Durban on sick leave.

27 *Powerful* calls at Ascension Island.
Terrible leaves Durban for China Station.
Death of Commandant-General Joubert.
Louis Botha succeeds him.

> *April*

3 *Powerful* calls at Las Palmas.

11 *Powerful* arrives at Portsmouth.

14 White arrives at Southampton.

19 Forbes sails from Durban for home.

24 White and *Powerful*'s crew attend public banquet at Portsmouth.

30 White received by Queen Victoria at Windsor.

> *May*

2 *Powerful*'s Naval Brigade received by Queen Victoria at Windsor.

5 Royal Academy Banquet: White and Lambton guests of honour.

7 *Powerful*'s Naval Brigade parades at the Horse Guards. Welcome by Mr Goschen and Prince of Wales. Receptions at Royal Exchange and Lloyds.

9 Buller resumes advance into Northern Natal.

15 Natal Army re-occupies Dundee.

16 Ian Forbes welcomed home to Rothiemay, Banffshire.

17 Relief of Mafeking.
Buller enters Newcastle.

18-
31 Naval Contingent with 4.7-in and 12-pr guns takes part in Royal Military Tournament, Agricultural Hall,

Islington, London.

24 Orange Free State formally annexed and renamed Orange River Colony.

30 President Kruger leaves Pretoria.

31 British forces occupy Johannesburg.

June

1 Boer Council at Pretoria resolve to continue guerrilla warfare.

5 Pretoria occupied.

Seventy-Five Years On

THE British who fell in South Africa in the war of 1899-1902 are not forgotten. The climate and terrain are such that those who died had to be buried on the spot, and of course their remains have not survived to this day. But many monuments were erected at the time by their comrades, some simple stone cairns, others more elaborate with inscriptions.

The South African Government has taken particular care to preserve these monuments to their former enemies. In some cases they remain on the spot where the man died, as on Wagon Hill, Ladysmith. Elsewhere Gardens of Remembrance have been established, where the monuments have been brought together, for example at Kimberley.

I am indebted for this information to Colonel Bertram Lang, late Argyll & Sutherland Highlanders. He served through the Boer War and First World War, retired in the 1930s, and only recently, at the age of 90, toured the South African battlefields.

As I glance back over these pages, one phrase above all others sticks in my memory: 'crackers at a picnic'. It was how Boer gunfire seemed to Ian Forbes in retrospect when, 14 years afterwards, he was under German fire at Ypres.

Now that three-quarters of a century have passed since the siege, the Boer War seems remote indeed. Yet at the time Ladysmith was a name to conjure with. A young newspaper correspondent with Buller's force described the beleaguered town as a '20-acre patch of tin houses and blue gum-trees,

137

but famous to the uttermost ends of the earth.' Flowery language by today's matter-of-fact standards of war reporting, yet truly Churchillian, and indeed from the pen of the master himself.

Churchill's despatches from Natal to the London 'Morning Post' were published in book form soon after the relief of Ladysmith. A young woman named Helen Compton presented a copy to her father for his birthday that year. Nine years later she was to marry a Ladysmith defender – Reynolds Sharp.

Between them the careers of those who went through the siege spanned the best part of a century of campaigning throughout the Empire: India at the time of the Mutiny, Afghanistan, Burma, the First Boer War, Egypt and two World Wars. To have studied and described these careers, however superficially, has been a stimulating experience; to have known the South African War Veterans and the descendants of the Ladysmith garrison members who have assisted me in the compilation of this book, has been a privilege.

APPENDIX I

Captain the Hon Hedworth Lambton   in command
Lieutenant F.G. Egerton   killed 2 November 1899
Lieutenant A.W. Heneage   12-pr battery
Lieutenant L. Halsey   Cove Redoubt & A Coy
Lieutenant M.H. Hodges   Junction Hill & B Coy.
Fleet Paymaster W.H.F. Kay   died of enteric on homeward
   passage
Surgeon J.G. Fowler
Engineer E.H. Ellis   gun mountings
Engineer C.C. Sheen   wounded 6 January, 1900
Gunner W. Sims   guns & mountings; later Junction Hill
   4.7-in gun
Midshipman J.R Middleton   A Coy.
Midshipman H.T. Hayes   A Coy.
Midshipman R.C. Hamilton   A.D.C. to Captain
Midshipman the Hon I.L.A. Carnegie   B Coy & 12-pr gun
   on Caesar's Camp
Midshipman Alick Stokes   12-pr gun battery
*Midshipman E.G. Chichester   B Coy.
*Midshipman C.R. Sharp   12-pr gun battery
*from HMS *Terrible*

OFFICERS ATTACHED
(joined the brigade after arrival at Ladysmith)

Lieutenant E.C. Tyndale-Biscoe   late R.N.
Lieutenant E. Stabb   died, enteric, 15 January, 1900

APPENDIX II

Lieutenant-Colonel W.H. Dick-Cunyngham, VC (Commanding Officer) wounded 21 October, 1899 and 6 January 1900. Died 7 January 1900.

Major W.A. Scott (Second in Command)

Major H.W.D. Denne   killed 21 October 1899

Major C.C. Miller-walnutt, DSO   killed 6 January 1900

Major H Wright   wounded 21 October 1899

Captain H.A. Bethune

Captain A.L.H. Buchanan   wounded 21 October 1899

Captain the Hon R.F. Carnegie   wounded 6 January 1900

Captain J.A.L. Haldane, DSO   wounded 21 October 1899
   prisoner November 1899

Captain C.F.N. Macready

*Captain T.B. Sellar (K.O.S.B.'s att.)

Captain E.C. Streatfield (Adjutant)

Captain G.S. Walker (R.A.M.C. att.)   died 24 February
   1900

Lieutenant W. Anderson (Quartermaster)

Lieutenant A.W.F. Baird

Lieutenant L.B. Bradbury   died 22 October 1899

Lieutenant I.A. Campbell   died 22 October 1899

Lieutenant C.W.M. Findlay   wounded 21 October 1899

Lieutenant I.R.I.F. Forbes

Lieutenant J.B. Gillatt (A & S.H. att.)

Lieutenant A.R. Hennessey (3rd Gordons att.)   wounded
   21 October 1899

Lieutenant W.W. MacGregor wounded 6 January 1900

Lieutenant A.H. Maclean (A & S.H. att.)

Lieutenant M.F. Meiklejohn   wounded 21 October 1899
Lieutenant C.G. Monro   killed 21 October 1899
Lieutenant Lord G. Stewart Murray (Bl. Watch)
Lieutenant L.B. Spencer (K.O.S.B's att.)

2nd Lieutenant A.A.D. Best   killed 4 July 1901
2nd Lieutenant J.K. Dick-Cunyngham
2nd Lieutenant the Hon R.G. Forbes
**2nd Lieutenant F.C.M. Maitland wounded 20 November 1899
2nd Lieutenant J.G.D. Murray   killed 21 October 1899

Notes

*   Captain Sellar came out to Ladysmith on his own initiative. After the siege he returned to his own corps, was charged with being absent without leave, and received no pay for the period.

**   2nd Lieutenant Maitland was the last officer to join the battalion, arriving on one of the last trains to reach Ladysmith before the siege.

APPENDIX III

Land Mountings for Naval Guns

ON 13 June 1900 Captain Percy Scott delivered a public lecture in Hong Kong on the mountings of the naval guns used both inside besieged Ladysmith and by the Ladysmith Relief Column. The following report of the occasion is taken from the special reprint of the lecture published by the *Hong Kong Daily Press:*

On 14 October the *Terrible* arrived at the Cape and found the campaign commenced, the Boers already across the Frontier, the British with insufficient troops to resist them, and their base 6,000 miles from the scene of operations.

Under these circumstances it was apparent that the Boers might invest Mafeking, Kimberley and Ladysmith, and then, having their base open, bring down from Pretoria long range guns against which field guns would be powerless.

I therefore took steps to see whether a mounting could be made which would enable the *Terrible*'s long range 12-prs to be used on shore to keep the Boer siege guns at a respectable distance. By the 21 October a mounting was made, tried, and found satisfactory. It consisted of a log of wood to form a trail, mounted on an axletree with a pair of ordinary Cape waggon wheels. On to this was placed the ship carriage, bolted down and secured in such a manner as not to interfere with it being put back on board should circumstances have required it; the necessity of this of course added to the difficulty in designing the mounting, a fact which perhaps my critics overlooked when they condemned it as clumsy.

On Wednesday, 25 October, General White in Ladysmith, finding that he had no artillery capable of keeping the Boer siege guns in check, wired to know if it were possible for

142

the Navy to send him some long-range 4.7 guns.

The Admiral asked me if I could design a mounting for a 4.7 and get two finished by the following afternoon. It was rather a rush, but they were ready by 5.00 pm, put on board the *Powerful* and she started with them, and four 12-pdrs for Durban. The mounting consisted of four pieces of timber, 14 feet long by 12 inches, placed in the form of a cross. On to the centre of this was placed the ordinary ship mounting bolted through to a plate underneath. The pedestal and timbers were thus all securely bolted together. Next, the gun-carriage was dropped over the spindle, and secured down by its clip plate. Subsequent experiments with a platform of this description showed that it was not even necessary to fill in round the timbers with earth; on firing, a slight jump of the platform, of course, took place, but this in itself was advantageous, as it relieved the strain.

The 4.7 guns used for the defence of Durban and subsequently sent to join General Buller's force at the front were on a different pattern of mounting to those hurriedly made for Ladysmith.

A double trail was used to allow of great elevation, and iron wheels were supplied. Each wheel consisted of a plate with a bush for the axletree in the centre, round the perimeter an angle iron on each side; outside of that a tyre was shrunk on.

A few strengthening strips were put on to the plate. A heavy axletree was supplied, on to which the double trail was secured and the carriage put on to it. Telescope sights were fitted. Six guns of this description of mounting were in use when I left: two with Lord Roberts, two with General Buller and two with General Gatacre.

They were easily travelled by a span of oxen, and were, I think, sufficiently mobile to accompany any column on the march.

By the end of November a good portion of the Ladysmith Relief Column had arrived and commenced to advance, the Naval Brigade, under Captain Jones, and Commander

Limpus with two 4.7 and 18 long 12 prs accompanying them. While the main Army was operating in the Spion Kop direction, General Barton was active at Chieveley and wanted a 4.7 on a railway truck to shell a new position occupied by the Boers.

There was no time to make a new mounting, so we put one of the platform mountings, similar to those sent to Ladysmith on a low truck, secured it down with chains and cut off the ends of the transverse baulks so as to allow it to pass through the tunnels.

Owing to the amount of energy absorbed by the hydraulic cylinders and the general elasticity of the mounting very little recoil was transmitted to the truck, and consequently the gun could be fired at right angles to the direction of the railway line.

As General Barton wished to have the alternative of using this gun off the truck if required, a little extra stability had to be given to compensate for the amount we had cut off the cross beams.

This was done by supplying a moveable beam which could be bolted on when the mounting was in situ. This was found a great advantage, as the platforms could then be sent intact by train instead of in pieces as was the case with those that went to Ladysmith.

Three more guns on this description of mounting were made and operated against the Boers at the final attack on Pieter's Hill.

In this final attack General Buller wanted still heavier ordnance, and wired to me, asking if I could possibly send him a 6-in gun. The telegram arrived on a Wednesday and the General expressed a wish to have it, if possible, by the following Monday, so there was not much time. A gun was taken out of the *Terrible*, and a design of a mounting prepared, the governing features of which were utility and a desire to comply with the General's wishes as regards time. It was finished on Sunday morning, and sent to the front. Some said that it was clumsy, others that it would fall to pieces the first round. It did not fall in pieces, but put upwards of 500 lyddite and common shell into the enemy's position, a fact which must have led them to regard it in more serious light than the view taken of it by a Member of Parliament, who referred to it as 'only picturesque.' A Boer prisoner, with whom I conversed, told me that they disliked this gun very much.

After the occupation of Ladysmith, General Buller, anticipating going north over the Biggarsberg, asked if I could, now that there was more time, supply a lighter and more mobile mounting for the 4.7-in gun; there was of course no difficulty in doing this. The heavy ship carriage was removed, and steel used instead of wood; a single wheel was placed in the rear between the trails to facilitate transport. When the extreme elevation of 370 was required, the rear wheel could be unshipped.

When firing with the wheel shipped, a locking arrangement was provided for keeping it in a fore and aft line. It was very mobile and I believe answered well. Four of them were made and turned over to the Royal Artillery.

No limbers were provided for any of these guns, the 6-in and 4.7 were travelled by a team of oxen, their ammunition coming along behind in an ordinary Cape waggon, the 12-prs for a short travel were up the tail of the waggon which carried their ammunition. For a long travel the gun was lifted out of its trunnions and put on to its waggon, with the ammunition, the whole not being an excessive weight for a team of oxen.

APPENDIX IV

At Sailor's Camp

(EXTRACT FROM 'THE STORY OF HMS POWERFUL')

THE camp of the *Powerful* Brigade at Ladysmith was pitched close to a hill on the south-east of the town. This hill came to be called 'Naval Brigade Hill.' Looking south-west from the guns, you could see the headquarters of General White in a mass of trees in front. Nearby, across the road, was the 'Field Printing Office', i.e. a wagon. 'Caesar's Camp', a ridge stormed by the Boers on 6 January 1900, could be seen on the left, and part of 'Maiden's Castle', another line of hills, on the right. Looking west, the camp of the 5th Lancers showed clearly to the right, while 'Wagon Hill' which the Boers carried on 6 January, but were forced to leave soon afterwards – was to the left and centre of the view. The camp of the Irish Fusiliers covering the Colenso road appeared far to the right.

A pathway marked by white stones led up the hillside to the Naval guns on 'Cove Redoubt.' The batteries were named 'Princess Victoria' and 'Lady Anne'. Lieutenant Halsey, RN, was in charge of the 4.7-in gun in 'Princess Victoria' battery.

Above the batteries was an elevated post called 'Gordon Hill', where Captain Lambton had his 'Conning Tower.' It was decidedly a land institution, but the officers and men disposed of all the features of the situation in battleship phrases. Here the Naval Brigade of the *Powerful* kept a look-out upon the Boers and directed the fire of their guns.

APPENDIX V

Naval Guns in Ladysmith

POWERFUL's brigade brought 10 guns of various calibres into the town, including four .45 Maxims, of which it is stated that only one was actually used, the others being 'merely ornaments to the earthworks on Gordon Hill' (between Observation Hill and Tunnel Hill. Thus there were seven effective Naval guns including the one Maxim. They are detailed below.

1. No.1 4.7-in quick-firing gun on Captain Scott's improvised wooden platform. Mounted on Cove Redoubt on 7 November and remained there throughout the siege.

2. No.2 4.7-in, specification as No.1. Initially mounted on Junction Hill (between Cove Redoubt and Tunnel Hill) on 2 November. Moved to Wagon Hill on 12 December but did not fire there. Returned to Junction Hill on 17 December. Moved back to Wagon Hill but not mounted in time for the attack of 6 January. Returned to Junction Hill on 10 January. Moved to the eastern end of Caesar's Camp on 26 February and remained there till the relief.

3. 12-pr Naval field gun. Initially on Gordon Hill, then on Junction Hill for the duration.

4. No.1 long-range 12-pr on Captain Scott's improvised field carriage. On Gordon Hill throughout the siege.

5. No.2 long-range 12-pr. Specification as No.1. Mounted on Gordon Hill until 27 November, then moved to Caesar's Camp.

6. No.3 long-range 12-pr. Specification as No.1. Mounted on Gordon Hill until 22 November, then moved to Cove Redoubt.

7. .45 Maxim. On Gordon Hill throughout the siege.

EXPENDITURE OF AMMUNITION

Guns	Rounds fired during battle of Lombard's Kop 30.10.99	Rounds fired during siege period	Total
4.7-in	46	514	560
12-pounders	98	784	882
3-pounders (Natal Naval Volunteers)		80	80
		1,378	1,522

Total of rounds fired by the Royal Artillery in Ladysmith was 9,680, including 4,624 during the siege period.

APPENDIX VI

Letters from Captain Lambton to Sir George White on the work of the Ladysmith Naval Brigade.

Naval Brigade Camp, Ladysmith,
11 January, 1900

SIR,

In compliance with your orders I have the honour to forward herewith a list of officers and men whom I wish to bring to your notice for services rendered.

Lieutenant Algernon W. Heneage, since the regrettable death of Lieutenant Frederick G. Egerton (who died on Thursday evening, 2nd November, 1899 from wounds received that morning when fighting his gun), has conducted the duties of Senior Executive Officer entirely to my satisfaction, and like all the officers and men under my command, was under constant shell fire during the first weeks of the investment.

Lieutenants Lionel Halsey and Michael H. Hodges have respectively been in command of the 4.7 guns at Cove Redoubt and Junction Hill, and have fought them with great skill and coolness, under, at times, a very accurate and plunging cross-fire from guns of much heavier calibre, especially at Lieutenant Hodges' gun, during the first fortnight.

The shooting of these guns has been brilliant, and it is generally accepted that the 6-inch gun at Pepworth Hill was eventually knocked out of action by Lieutenant Hodges' gun, at a range of 7,000 yards, to the great relief of the inhabitants of Ladysmith, and though the same good fortune has not attended the firing of the Cove Redoubt gun at the

6-inch gun on Bulwana, yet the emplacement of the latter gun has been repeatedly struck by its fire, and many of the enemy killed and wounded, at a range varying according to the wind and temperature, from 8,200 to 8,900 yards, which shows the nicety of calculation required.

Retired Lieutenant Edward C. Tyndale Biscoe, RN, who handsomely volunteered his services on 1 November 1899, has been of the greatest assistance to me, his experience in the Soudan, 1884, and Matabele, 1893 to 1897 campaigns, rendering him a very valuable and reliable officer.

Lieutenant Edward Stabb, RNR, also volunteered his services, which I gladly accepted, the necessary distribution of my guns rendering me very short of officers, and I found him very useful.

The experience gained by Fleet Paymaster William H.F. Kay, in Abyssinia, on the Nile, and in Burmah, has enabled him to look after the Commissariat and comforts of the Naval Camp, with activity, facility, and ability.

Surgeon James G. Fowler has been most assiduous in his attendance and duties towards the sick, of which, unfortunately, there has been a heavy percentage.

Engineers Edgar H. Ellis and Charles C. Sheen have rendered most valuable and arduous services in the mounting of the 4.7 guns, Mr Ellis being stationed at and sharing the fighting of the 4.7 gun at Cove Redoubt, previously mentioned.

Mr Sheen has erected three condensers at the railway station, whereby 6,000 gallons of distilled water are supplied daily to the troops.

He also was one of the party under Mr Sims, gunner, employed in mounting the 4.7 gun on Waggon Hill, on Saturday, 6 January, and was actively engaged all that day in the defence of that position against the Boers, receiving a slight wound in the face from a shrapnel shell.

Mr Sims, gunner, is a most capable and indefatigable officer, and of great ability. I understand his gallant services on Waggon Hill, 6 January, have been reported to you by

150

Colonel Hamilton.

Messrs John R. Middleton, Henry T. Hayes, Robert C. Hamilton, Hon Ian L.A. Carnegie, Alick Stokes, Edward G. Chichester, and Charles R. Sharp, midshipmen, have all behaved with great coolness under fire, and satisfactorily carried out the duties allotted to them.

Mr Carnegie has had charge of a 12-pr gun at Caesar's Camp since 27 November 1899, which he has fought successfully under, at times, a hot fire.

All the Petty Officers and men have behaved well both in action and in carrying out the various duties connected with the defence of the position assigned to the Naval Brigade; but I specially mention the following, who, being captains of guns, have had the best opportunities of distinguishing themselves for coolness under fire:-

Henry W.C. Lee, PO, 1st class, captain of 4.7 gun at Junction Hill and Waggon Hill.

Philip T. Sisk, PO, 1st class, captain of 4.7 gun, Cove Redoubt.

Archibald C. Pratt, leading seaman, 12-pr, Leicester Post.

Albert G. Withers, PO, 1st class, 12-pr, Gordon Post.

Samuel E. Hemmings, leading seaman, 12-pr, Manchester Camp.

Lee, in addition, was specially noticeable for his gallant behaviour at Waggon Hill, on Saturday, 6 January, himself shooting a Boer, whilst assisting in the retaking of the hill.

I have, etc.,
H. LAMBTON, Captain, RN

Lieutenant-General Sir George White, VC, GCB, etc. Commanding at Ladysmith.

REPORT OF PROCEEDINGS OF NAVAL BRIGADE DURING BOER ATTACK ON LADYSMITH, SATURDAY, 6 JANUARY 1900

Naval Brigade Camp, Ladysmith,
8 January, 1900.

SIR,

At 2.45 am, on Saturday, 6th January, a heavy rifle fire was heard at Waggon Hill, which gradually extended right along Caesar's Camp.

2 At daybreak the enemy's artillery commenced a heavy fire from all positions, which was kept up until sunset.

The Naval guns under my command engaged the Boer batteries as heavily as the small amount of remaining ammunition permitted.

The 4.7 gun on Cove Redoubt, under Lieutenant Lionel Halsey, fired 28 rounds at the Bulwana 6-inch gun, making excellent practice at 8,500 yards, and repeatedly striking the parapet; this accurate fire was probably the cause of the poor shooting by this 6-inch gun at our Field Artillery, who were posted on the plain below Caesar's Camp, and were shelling the Boers who had occupied the extreme south-east end of that position.

3 The 12-pr at Gordon Post also engaged Bulwana, and the hill beyond Caesar's Camp, where the Boers' reinforcements were supposed to be collecting, but the range was too great to be really effective.

4 The 12-pr at Leicester Post fired at the enemy's 12-pr on Rifleman Ridge, and also at the 4.5 gun on Surprise Hill, making good practice at the latter, and placing one shell right into the embrasure.

5 The 12-pr on Caesar's Camp in charge of the Hon Ian Carnegie, midshipman, was actively engaged during the day with the enemy's guns on Middle Hill, and to the left of Flat-topped Hill, making good shooting, and receiving a hot fire in return, one shell bursting in the embrasure, without, however, doing any harm.

6 The 4.7 gun from Junction Hill was taken over late on Friday night to be mounted in a new position on Waggon Hill, but before this could be accomplished, the enemy's attack commenced, and the gun's crew, under Mr Sims, gunner, accompanied by Mr Sheen, engineer, participated in the defence of that position under Colonel Ian Hamilton during the day.

I have, etc.

H. LAMBTON, Captain, RN

Lieutenant-General Sir George White, VC, GCB, etc
Commanding at Ladysmith

Ladysmith,
28 February, 1900.

SIR,

I HAVE the honour to report that the *Powerful*'s Naval Brigade, consisting of 283 officers and men, two 4.7, three 12-pr, one 12-pr 8 cwt, and four Maxim guns, landed at Durban, Sunday evening, 29 October and arrived here in two special trains about 8.30 Monday morning.

The battle of Lombard's Kop was then in progress. Fifty spans of oxen were obtained for the long 12-prs, and after consultation with Colonel Knox, RA, CB, I proceeded with them, and a company of bluejackets in support, to a position about half a mile to the west of Limit Hill.

However, before arriving there, the order for the left of the line to fall back was received, and during the slow return along the Newcastle Road, the teams of oxen afforded a tempting target to the Pepworth gun, which, after about half a dozen good shots, burst a shell under the leading gun, overturning it and disabling the gun's crew, and stampeding the cattle and drivers.

Fresh oxen were obtained, and the gun brought in.

In the meantime, the other two 12-prs took up a position

on the flats in front of Gordon Post, and opened fire on the Pepworth gun at a range of about 7,000 yards, making good practice, and the Boer gun soon ceased firing for the day.

Gordon Post was assigned for the Naval Brigade to hold, and the 12-prs and Maxims were distributed along that position.

November 1st, one 4.7 gun was mounted at Junction Hill, and the other on Cove Redoubt on Friday, 3 November.

During the progress of the siege some variations in the disposition of the guns became necessary; amongst others, one 12-pr being permanently stationed on Caesar's Camp, and the Junction Hill 4.7 gun being occasionally moved to Wagon Hill, and finally to Caesar's Camp, to meet the probable moves of the enemy.

I have already, in my letter of January recommending officers and men to your notice, entered into details of the expenditure of ammunition and the damage believed to have been done to the enemy by my guns, and have nothing further to add.

The conduct of the brigade has been excellent.

I regret that, in common with the large majority of the regiments of the garrison, there has been much sickness amongst my officers and men, 2 officers and 25 men having succumbed to wounds and disease, chiefly enteric and dysentery.

To have had the good fortune to participate in your memorable defence of Ladysmith will always be a pride to the *Powerful*'s Naval Brigade, and on behalf of my officers and men I take this opportunity of expressing my recognition of the cordial kindness we have received from the gallant army under your distinguished command.

I have, etc,
H. LAMBTON, Captain, RN

Lieutenant-General Sir George White, VC, GCB, etc.
Commanding at Ladysmith.

APPENDIX VII

Sir George White's Despatch

IN an official Despatch dated 23 March 1900 and addressed to the Chief of Staff to the Field-Marshal Commanding-in-Chief in South Africa (Lord Kitchener), Sir George White referred in the following terms to *Powerful*'s brigade.

'Captain the Hon Hedworth Lambton, RN, commanding the Naval Brigade, reached Ladysmith in the nick of time, when it became evident that I was not strong enough to meet the enemy in the open field. He brought with him two 4.7-in and four 12-pr guns which proved to be the only ordnance in my possession capable of equalling in range the enemy's heavy guns. Although the ammunition available was very limited, Captain Lambton so economised it that it lasted out till the end of the siege, and under his direction the naval guns succeeded in keeping at a distance the enemy's siege guns, a service which was of the utmost importance. Captain Lambton personally has been the life of the garrison throughout the siege.'

APPENDIX VIII

Naval Brigade
Awards – Promotions – Casualties

All members of *Powerful*'s Ladysmith Brigade were entitled to the South African Campaign Medal with 'Defence of Ladysmith' clasp.

Captain the Hon Hedworth Lambton was made a Companion of the Order of the Bath.

PROMOTIONS

Lieutenant F.G. Egerton promoted to Commander after being mortally wounded.

Engineer E.H. Ellis ⎫ to be Chief Engineers
Engineer C.C. Sheen ⎭

Gunner W. Sims to be Lieutenant RN.

Surgeon J.G. Fowler was noted for early promotion.

The Midshipmen were recommended for early promotion on qualifying for the rank of Lieutenant.

GUN CAPTAINS SPECIALLY MENTIONED IN DESPATCHES

Petty Officer H.C.W. Lee, Captain of 4.7 on Junction Hill.

Petty Officer P.T. Sisk, Captain of 4.7 at Cove Redoubt.

Leading Seaman A.C. Pratt, Captain of 12-pounder at Leicester Post.

Petty Officer A.G. Withers, Captain of 12-pounder at Gordon Post.

Leading Seaman S.E. Hemming, Captain of 12-pounder at Manchester Camp.

CASUALTIES

	Officers	Men
Killed or died of wounds	1	5
Died of disease	2	25
Wounded	1	4

156

2nd Bn Gordon Highlanders Honours and Decorations

VICTORIA CROSS
Captain M.F. Meiklejohn
Regimental Sergeant Major W. Robertston
for gallantry at Elandslaagte

C.B.
Lieutenant Colonel W.A. Scott

D.S.O.
Majors H. Wright, Hon F. Gordon
Captains E.C. Streatfield, A.W.F. Baird
Lieutenants J.R.E. Stansfield, J.K. Dick-Cunyngham
brevets Bt.-Lieutenant Colonel: Major C.F.N. Macready
Bt.-Lieutenant Colonel on promotion to Major: Captain J.A.L. Haldane
Bt.-Major: Captains H.A. Bethune, Hon R.F. Carnegie
Hon Captain Q-M & Hon Lieutenant W. Anderson

D.C.M.
CS's H. Powell, W. J.D. Pryce,
Drum-Major G. Lawrence, Pipe-Major J. Dunbar,
Pipe-Cpl. K. MacLeod, Cpl. C. Macdonald,
Drummer J. May.

Other Military Units in Ladysmith

REGULAR ARMY

1st Devons
5th Dragoon Guards
1st Gloucesters
18th Hussars
19th Hussars
1st King's Royal Rifles
2nd King's Royal Rifles
5th Lancers
1st Leicesters
1st Liverpools
1st Manchesters
2nd Rifle Brigade
1st Royal Irish Fusiliers
Army Ordnance Dept.
Army Service Corps.
Army Veterinary Dept.
Royal Army Medical Corps.
Royal Engineers

ROYAL ARTILLERY

I. Brigade: 13th, 67th, 69th Batteries
II. Brigade: 21st, 42nd, 53rd Batteries
4th Mountain Battery
63rd Howitzer Battery

COLONIAL VOLUNTEERS

Border Mounted Rifles
Imperial Light Horse

Natal Carbineers
Natal Mounted Rifles
Natal Naval Volunteers
Natal Volunteer Brigade

The Royal Tournament
a Link with Percy Scott and Ladysmith

THE Royal Navy Field Gun Competition, that ever-popular feature of the annual Royal Tournament at Earl's Court, London, held in aid of Service charities, was the brain-child of Percy Scott.

It started as a mock-battle staged at the Gunnery School, Portsmouth, (HMS *Excellent*) for a visit of the Lords of the Admiralty. The display was later transferred to London as part of an exhibition to raise funds for the orphans and widows of sailors who had lost their lives in the service of their country.

While the campaign for the relief of Ladysmith was still in progress the organisers of the 1900 Tournament, then held at the Royal Agricultural Hall, Islington, asked the Navy to provide 80 seamen for the occasion and one 4.7-in gun fitted with Captain Scott's mounting 'as used at Ladysmith.'

The Captain, HMS *Excellent*, replied that such a mounting would cost between £50 and £100. The first reaction of the Tournament organisers was that the cost was prohibitive. However, there must have been a change of heart, as in the event the Naval Tournament Party brought two 4.7-in guns to London. They detrained at Nine Elms Station on 15 May, from where the guns were drawn through the streets by eight horses of Guards Transport and, as the log records, 'in places a very large crowd had collected and the police and cavalry escort were most necessary to prevent them breaking through.'

On the afternoon of 17 May a dress rehearsal of the gun display was attended by about 100 reporters and 3,000

children from various charity schools. On the following day
the Tournament was officially opened by HRH the Prince of
Wales. The Naval Brigade provided a guard of honour
outside the hall.

Glossary

Donga *River bed, often dry*
Drift *Ford through a river*
Fontein *Spring*
Klip *Stone or diamond*
Kopje *Small hill*
Kraal *Native village*
Krantz *Valley or cleft between two hills*
Laager *Boer encampment*
Mealies *Maize*
Nek *Saddle connecting two hills*
Pont *Ferry*
Poort *Pass between hills*
Rand *Ridge*
Sangar *Fortification of loose stones or boulders*
Spruit *Ditch on the veldt*
Stoep *Verandah*
Veldt *Open pasture-land*

BIBLIOGRAPHY

Amery, L.S. (Ed.) 'The Times' History of the War in South Africa.

Atkins, J.B. The Relief of Ladysmith.

Buckle, G.E. (Ed.) The Letters of Queen Victoria, 3rd Series, Vol.III.

Burne, Lieut. C.R.N. With the Naval Brigade in Natal.

Churchill, W.S. London to Ladysmith via Pretoria.

Crowe, G. The Commission of HMS *Terrible*.

Dickson, W.K.L. The Biograph in Battle.

Durand, Sir M. The Life of Sir George White.

Farrar-Hockley, A. "Goughie" (General Sir Hubert Gough)

Gardner, Brian The Lion's Cage.

Gardner, Brian Mafeking, A Victorian Legend.

Greenhill-Gardyne, A.D. The Life of a Regiment – the Gordon Highlanders, Vol.III.

Headlam, J. History of the Royal Artillery, Vols.II & III.

Holt, Edgar. The Boer War.

Jacson, M. The Record of a Regiment of the Line – 1st Devons, 1899-1902.

Jeans, Surgeon T.T. Naval Brigades in the South African War.

Macready, Sir N. Annals of an Active Life.

Mahan, Capt. A.T. The Story of the War in South Africa.

Maurice, Sir F.B. The Life of Lord Rawlinson of Trent.

Maurice, Sir J.F. History of the War in South Africa.

Nevinson, H.W. Ladysmith, Diary of a Siege.

Padfield, P.T. Aim Straight.

Pearse, H.H.S. Four Months Besieged.

Scott, Sir P. Fifty Years in the Royal Navy.

Selby, John. The Boer War.

Steevens, G.W. From Capetown to Ladysmith.

Symons, Julian. Buller's Campaign.
Anonymous. HMS *Powerful*.
Anonymous. An Absent-Minded War.

GOVERNMENT WHITE PAPERS

Cmd.457 & 458, 1901: South Africa Despatches.
Cmd.1789-1792, 1903: Royal Commission on the War in
  South Africa.